Great Restaurants Cookbook, U.S.A.

ADER VIC'S Marzetti's GENE
LOBSTE
HOUS

NDEL'S Karl Ratzsch's

izona Inn MAXIM'S Lüchow'

Danny's Au de PARIS Putsch's 210 ive
PETIT anc
JEAN Tony's SEÑOR

Pontchartrain
Wine Cellars LONGFELLOW

GGS Rod's Shadowbrook Wayside Inn

rimos Perditas BLACK BASS HO
Poor Richard's Ta
hoyt's Ben Gross Kungshol.
The DINNER BELL
ustines LONDON CHOP HOUSE

BARBETTA Sun Valley Lo

sgow Arms CHEZ The Len
LOUIS Jackson La
cchanal The Spanish Pavilion
THE NATIONS INT

OLL GATE LODGE Hanalei Plantation

Maitre Jacques Russian Tea Room

THE BLUE HORSE

Mario's of Dallas La fonda KON-TIKI

RNIE'S Northstar Inn THE SeaGu

D STONE INN Campbell's Heritage Hil

CO Great Restaurants Baroqu

Cookbook, U.S.A. Indi

The Drake LA MEDITERRANEE

Pirates' House QVORVM Jock

Clu

The CAFÉ JOHNELL Zodia

mon House

Greenbrier **A Rutledge Book / Grosset & Dunlap** Pavilion Johnn

Tree The Golden Lion The Bakery and

odge Look's Brennan's Kay

Omar Khayyam's

IONAL RESTAURANT Swiss Hütte Cellar

Publisher	*Fred R. Sammis*
Supervising Editor	*Stephanie Stefanssen*
Editor	*Doris Townsend*
Art Director	*Allan Mogel*
Editorial Production	*Marilyn Weber*
Associate Editor	*Therese Pol*
Art Associate	*Gwen McLoone*

Photography   *Stan LoPresto*
and Tom O'Keefe, Show Associates, Inc.

Home Economist   *Helen Feingold*

Published by
Rutledge Books, Inc.
17 East 45th Street
New York, New York 10017

Library of Congress Catalog Card Number 69-17722

Distributed by Grosset & Dunlap, Inc.

Flatware courtesy of Sterling Silversmiths'
Guild of America
China courtesy of Lenox, Inc.
Page 58: photo taken at Churchill Apartments
Page 72: accessories by Bonniers, New York
Page 98: table setting by S. Wyler, New York
Page 114: table setting by Bonniers, New York
Page 118: accessories by Surma, New York

On the front cover:
Perdrix Vallée d'Auge—The Cellar

On the back cover:
Fresh Stuffed Artichoke—Jackson Lake
Lodge ; Pompano en Papillote—Cape
Cod Room; Flounder Mornay—Justines

Printed in Italy by Mondadori, Verona

Great Restaurants Cookbook, U.S.A.

CONTENTS

INTRODUCTION

Fine dining is a fine art—one not practiced exclusively by great restaurants. Between a magnificent dinner expertly served and beautifully presented and a patched-together meal put carelessly on the table there are many degrees of difference. These differences, traditionally, are the result of time and patience. Great expertise is not required; anyone who is able to read can cook well, provided he or she is blessed with a little of that priceless attribute known as flair. But now even time and patience are not as necessary as once they were. For this is the day of truly useful, truly valid shortcuts—without short-cutting quality—through the use of convenience foods. One of the most versatile of these foods, Campbell's Soups, can be used in a countless number of interesting, delicious dishes. Indeed, there's very little that these soups won't enhance from the point of view of flavor, ease of preparation, and economy of time.

One, two, or even three of these condensed soups permit easy-to-prepare variations on the standard sauces so much a part of good cooking—and such stumbling blocks for the average cook.

All of the interesting and unusual recipes in this book are prepared with the use of these soups. All are adaptations of the *spécialités de la maison* of restaurants famous for their food, their service, their ambience. These are the truly great, the honored, the sought-out restaurants in all parts of the country. They are top award winners, restaurants that know all the secrets of classic cookery.

Some of the recipes in this book, though elegant indeed, are quickly and easily prepared. Some require a bit more time and patience—but less of either of those two precious commodities than

when made the longer way. With the use of condensed soups, which are a combination of already prepared ingredients, these recipes are easily made.

In using this book, adhere to good-cooking practices: measure carefully with standard measuring utensils, and always level; preheat oven or broiler; never cook at a temperature higher than the one specified; read the recipe in advance to make certain all ingredients will be on hand when you are ready to prepare the dish.

Some of the recipes call for already prepared items—a batch of crêpes, for example, a brown sauce, a sauce suprême—without providing the method. The recipe occurs elsewhere in the book; a consultation of the index will tell you where.

Here is a book to serve you in several ways. It will guide you in preparing dishes that will earn you a reputation as a fabulous cook. It will guide you to the best of restaurants in your own city or when you travel. It will help you plan an important part of your vacation pleasure—the enjoyment of elegant food, meticulously served in beautiful surroundings. We tell you something about each restaurant—how much will depend on the length of the recipes we give you from that particular restaurant. The book also provides a section on Table Settings to stir your imagination when you want to serve food as beautifully as you have cooked it. And for those who find French and Italian menus something of a struggle—and who doesn't —there is a section of Menu French, Menu Italian terms—a glossary to make you comfortable in finding your way around Continental menus.

We hope that you will enjoy this book, use it often, and treasure it as a friend.

—The Editors

Au Petit Jean

In the heart of the lush looking-glass community of Beverly Hills—where the per capita income is the highest in the world—is Au Petit Jean. Providing French food in the grand manner for a sophisticated clientele that likes its dining, like the rest of its life-style, truly elegant, Au Petit Jean has been distinguished by many awards. Presided over by Maître d'hôtel-Manager Sebastian, it is recognized as one of the finest French restaurants in the country. Here, in a quietly glamorous atmosphere, superb food, fine wines, and deft service combine to create exceptional meals—and memories —for the fortunate visitor to the California of towering palm trees, manicured landscapes and Rolls-Royces. Dinner at Au Petit Jean is an experience to be treasured.

Duckling à l'Orange
Serves 4

1 duckling, 4½ to 5 pounds
1 can (10½ ounces) condensed beef broth
1 cup orange juice
¼ cup Cointreau or Grand Marnier
2 tablespoons cornstarch
1 tablespoon honey
1 teaspoon lemon juice
1 tablespoon orange rind, cut in thin strips

On rack in a shallow baking pan, roast duckling at 325°F. for 2 to 2½ hours (about 30 minutes per pound). Meanwhile, in saucepan, combine remaining ingredients except orange rind. Cook until thickened, stirring constantly. Remove duck; pour off fat. Stir sauce into drippings in pan. Add orange rind; heat. Cut duckling into serving-size pieces; arrange on serving platter. Pour part of sauce over duckling; serve remaining sauce. Garnish with orange sections and cherries.

Left: Duckling à l'Orange

Foie de Veau Sauté à la Vénitienne
Calves' Liver in Wine Sauce
Serves 4

1 pound calves' liver, cut into ½-inch-thick slices
Salt, pepper
Flour
¼ cup butter
2 tablespoons Marsala wine
1 can (10½ ounces) condensed onion soup
2 teaspoons cornstarch mixed with
2 tablespoons water

Sprinkle liver slices with salt and pepper. Dredge liver slices with flour. Melt butter in a large skillet. Sauté liver slices until brown on both sides and the desired degree of doneness. Remove liver to a platter and keep warm. Stir Marsala and onion soup into pan drippings. Stir in cornstarch mixture. Cook over low heat, stirring constantly until sauce bubbles and thickens. Spoon sauce over liver.

Adaptations from recipes by Food and Beverage Director Paul Gribi.

The Bakery

The Bakery is the unpretentious name of what started out some years ago as an unpretentious store-front restaurant on Chicago's Near North Side. Hungarians soon learned that Owner-Chef Louis Szathmary had a superlative way with their native specialties; they were swiftly followed by everyone else addicted to outstanding Continental cuisine. With renown, The Bakery's setting has gained a certain luster, but it remains intimate and subordinate to the management's real business: epicurean dining. There is no printed menu. Diners (who must be knowledgeable enough to have reserved several days in advance; there are never any free tables) simply put themselves into the dedicated hands of Chef Louis, who still personally prepares —and often helps to serve—each day's selection of glorious five-course dinners.

Flemish Carbonnades
Serves 4 to 6

1½ pounds round steak, sliced ¾ inch thick
2 tablespoons shortening
¾ cup beer
1 can (10½ ounces) condensed onion soup
2 teaspoons sugar
1 tablespoon flour mixed with ¼ cup water

Cut meat into serving-size pieces; pound with meat mallet. In a skillet, brown meat in shortening; pour off fat. Add beer; stir to loosen browned bits in pan. Add soup and sugar. Cover; cook over low heat for 1 hour, stirring now and then. Stir flour mixture into pan. Slowly cook, stirring constantly, until thickened and smooth. Makes about 1 cup of gravy.

Hungarian Whitefish with Mushrooms and Sour Cream
Serves 4

4 boneless whitefish fillets
¼ cup butter
Salt, paprika
1 cup sliced mushrooms
1 can (10½ ounces) condensed cream of mushroom soup
1 cup sour cream
Paprika

Butter a shallow baking dish large enough to hold fish fillets in a single layer. Place fillets in dish and dot with butter. Sprinkle fish with salt and paprika. Sprinkle mushrooms over fish fillets. Bake in a preheated 350° F. oven for 15 minutes. Combine soup and sour cream. Heat just until mixture bubbles. Spoon sauce over fish and bake an additional 15 minutes or until fish flakes. Sprinkle top with paprika. Top with additional spoonful of sour cream, if desired.

Left: Flemish Carbonnades

Adapted by Owner-Chef Louis Szathmary.

Cherry Glaze for Ham

1 can (1 pound) sour cherries packed in water
2 tablespoons cornstarch
¼ cup red wine
1 can (10½ ounces) condensed chicken broth

Drain cherries and reserve juice. Put juice and half of the cherries into a blender and whirl until smooth. Stir purée into cornstarch. Stir in wine and chicken broth. Cook over low heat, stirring constantly, until thick. Stir in cherries that were left whole. Spoon hot sauce over slices of baked ham or sautéed ham slices. Makes about 3 cups of sauce.

Tomato Stuffed with Flounder Fillet
Serves 4

4 firm, ripe tomatoes
Salt, pepper
1 pound flounder fillet, each fillet cut lengthwise
into 2 long strips
1 can (10½ ounces) condensed cream of
asparagus soup
1 cup sour cream

Core tomatoes and cut into halves, top to bottom. Scoop out about half of the pulp. Sprinkle tomatoes with salt and pepper. Roll up strips of fish and place a roll, spiral side up, in each tomato. Sprinkle with salt and pepper. Combine soup and sour cream. Spoon over filled tomatoes. Place tomatoes into a shallow casserole. Bake for 35 minutes in a preheated 350° F. oven until tomatoes are tender and fish flakes easily. Serve garnished with pitted black olives.

Turkey Divan
Serves 4

½ pound sliced cooked turkey
1 package (10 ounces) frozen broccoli spears,
cooked and drained
1 can (10½ ounces) condensed cream of
chicken soup
4 slices American cheese

Brush 4 individual casseroles with butter. Place turkey slices at bottom. Top with broccoli spears. Spoon soup over broccoli. Place cheese slice over soup. Bake in a preheated 450° F. oven for 15 minutes or until cheese is melted and bubbly.

Fruits de Mer en Croûte
Serves 6

1 package pie-crust mix
1 can (7 ounces) tuna, drained
1 can (1 pound) salmon, skin and bones removed
1 can (10½ ounces) condensed cream of
mushroom soup
2 eggs, well beaten
½ cup dry bread crumbs
1 egg yolk, beaten
1 tablespoon water

Sauce

1 can (10½ ounces) condensed cream of
mushroom soup
⅓ cup light cream

Prepare pie crust according to package directions. Roll out on a lightly floured board to an oblong 14 x 10 inches. Combine tuna, salmon, soup, eggs, and crumbs. Blend well and spoon fish in a loaf shape down the center of the oblong crust, making the loaf 12 inches long. Wrap dough around fish; seal edges with water. Place seam side down on greased cookie sheet. With scissors, cut off the two corners at one end of the loaf to shape the fish's head. With a blunt knife draw lines for eye and gills. Slash dough at other end to resemble the fish's tail. Brush entire fish with 1 egg yolk beaten with 1 tablespoon water. With scissors points, make V-shaped cuts in the fish to resemble scales. Bake in a preheated 425° F. oven for 40 minutes or until fish is richly browned. Combine soup and cream. Heat until bubbly. Cut fish pie into slices and spoon mushroom sauce over each serving.

14

Arizona Inn

Tucson offers an ideal combination of elements for residents and visitors alike: informal Western living, magnificent scenery in the surrounding desert and mountains, and a cosmopolitan culture to satisfy the most demanding. The Spanish flag was the first to fly over the city that was built to withstand Apache Indian attacks. And before Arizona came into the Union in 1912, the city flew the flags of Mexico and the Confederate States. One of the pleasures of vacationing in Tucson is staying—or at least dining if the Inn is full—at the Arizona Inn, three miles from the center of town. The Inn is a luxurious resort hotel, whose beautifully landscaped gardens provide a picturesque setting for the pink stucco buildings. Buffet luncheons are served at the pool; indoor buffet suppers are a Sunday feature. The menu offers a wide choice of gourmet dishes, some prepared to individual tastes. Open in season only.

Braised Short Ribs of Beef Ménagère

Serves 6

6 pounds short ribs
Salt, pepper
1 carrot, minced
¼ cup each minced celery, onion
2 cloves garlic, chopped
½ cup dry red wine
4 whole cloves
2 bay leaves
4 cans (10¾ ounces each) condensed tomato soup
3 cans (10½ ounces each) condensed
beef broth

Cut short ribs into serving-size pieces and trim all excess fat. Sprinkle meat with salt and pepper. Place ribs in a shallow pan and brown in a preheated 400° F. oven for 30 minutes. Lower heat to 350° F. Add carrot, celery, onion, garlic, wine, cloves, bay leaves, and soups. Cover pan and bake in a 350° F. oven for about 1 hour. Uncover and bake 1 more hour. When tender, remove ribs from the pan to a serving platter; skim all excess fat from the sauce. Strain the sauce; thicken, if desired, with flour mixed with water. Spoon hot sauce over ribs. Serve with egg noodles.

Cold Monterey Avocado Soup

Serves 6 to 8

2 ripe medium avocados
3 cups light cream
1 can (10½ ounces) condensed cream of
chicken soup
Dash Worcestershire sauce
½ teaspoon salt
¼ teaspoon pepper
Sprinkle ground nutmeg
¼ teaspoon MSG

Mix together all ingredients except avocados and chill well. Just before serving, peel avocados and remove seeds. Press through a sieve or whirl in a blender. Stir in previously mixed and chilled ingredients and blend well. Serve garnished with chopped chives.

Adapted by Chef Hans Jordi.

BARBETTA

When Barbetta opened in 1906 on New York's burgeoning West Side, it was unique in a city already crowded with Italian restaurants because it served the north Italian food of Piemonte. Gourmets still consider it the only truly Piemontese restaurant in the country, and the quality of its food remains superb. But in other ways it has changed. It is no longer the down-to-earth, bare-floored rendezvous where such notables as Caruso, Toscanini, and Pinza foregathered for serious dining. Celebrities still flock here, as do theatergoers with enough time to do justice to the cuisine. But they dine now in a setting of dramatic Old-World splendor created by Laura Maioglio, daughter of the founder—a setting that, in combination with the wonderful food and fine wines from Barbetta's own vineyards in Piemonte, makes each meal here an unforgettable pleasure, even for those with firsthand memories of Piemonte itself.

Baby Pheasant in Casserole

Serves 4 to 6

2 young pheasants
Black pepper
2 tablespoons shortening or *bacon drippings*
Pinch rosemary, crushed
Pinch sage
1 bay leaf, crumbled
½ cup shredded carrot
½ cup finely diced celery
1 can (10½ ounces) condensed onion soup
½ pound small whole white onions

Sprinkle pheasants lightly with pepper. In Dutch oven or flameproof casserole, brown pheasants in shortening, with rosemary, sage, and bay leaf. Remove pheasants. Cook carrot and celery for a few minutes in drippings; stir in soup. Replace pheasants; add onions. Cover. Cook over low heat about 1 hour or until pheasants are tender. Place pheasants on warm serving platter. Garnish with watercress or parsley. Spoon fat off gravy. Thicken if desired with a small amount of cornstarch or flour, dissolved in twice the amount of water. Cook, stirring, until the gravy bubbles and is thickened.

Risotto alla Piemontese

Rice with Chicken Livers

Serves 4 to 6

1 cup rice
3 chicken livers, cut up
⅓ cup dried wild mushrooms, soaked 1 hour
⅓ cup chopped onion
¼ cup butter or *margarine*
2 cans (10½ ounces each) condensed chicken broth
Parmesan cheese

In saucepan, brown rice and cook livers, mushrooms, and onion in butter until tender. Add broth. Cover; bring to a boil. Cook over low heat 20 minutes or until all liquid is absorbed. Serve with cheese.

Left: Baby Pheasant in Casserole

Adaptations from recipes by Owner Laura Maioglio.

Baroque

New York's elegant East Side is lined with charming small restaurants, but the romantic intimacy of Baroque gives it a particular magic. Keyed by the famous baroque mural on its wall, Baroque is a haven of subdued luxury. Marvelous for dinner, it can be a little dangerous for lunch, when the unwary visitor may find himself beguiled into lingering far too long over the fine French food, served with Continental expertise and made even more appealing with French wines from an excellent list.

Carré of Lamb Sarladaise
Rack of Lamb with Truffle Sauce
Serves 4

1 rack of lamb, about 4 pounds
Salt, pepper, crumbled rosemary
4 medium Idaho potatoes
¼ cup butter
1 can (⅞ ounce) truffles
⅓ cup white wine
1 can (10½ ounces) condensed beef broth
2 tablespoons flour mixed with ¼ cup water

Sprinkle lamb with salt, pepper, and crumbled rosemary. Roast on a rack in a shallow pan in a preheated 350°F. oven for 1 hour or until lamb is just done. Slice potatoes very thinly and dry well. Melt butter in a large skillet. Arrange slices of potato in skillet in layers. Slice half of the truffles and add to the potatoes. Cook until brown on one side, turn and brown on other side. In another skillet combine remaining truffles which have been chopped, white wine, and beef broth. Stir flour mixture into broth. Cook over low heat, stirring constantly, until sauce bubbles and thickens. Carve lamb into slices. Serve slices of lamb with hot sauce and potatoes.

Left: Carré of Lamb Sarladaise

Bitock à la Russe
Veal-Chicken Patties with Asparagus Sauce
Serves 4

1 whole chicken breast,
skinned and boned
½ pound ground raw veal
1 cup soft white bread crumbs
½ cup heavy cream
1 small onion, chopped
½ teaspoon salt
¼ teaspoon pepper
⅛ teaspoon ground nutmeg
¼ cup butter
1 can (10½ ounces) condensed cream of
asparagus soup
½ cup light cream

Chop raw chicken very fine and mix with veal, bread crumbs, heavy cream, onion, salt, pepper, and nutmeg. Shape mixture into 4 patties. Fry patties in ¼ cup butter until golden brown on both sides. Add soup and light cream and simmer slowly until mixture is heated through—but do not allow the sauce mixture to boil.

Adaptations from recipes by Owner George Bugoni.

BIGGS RESTAURANT

When the massive, brass-trimmed door of Biggs, in Chicago, swings silently open, the visitor enters not merely into the plush and softly lit interior of a great town house but into another century. Housed in the gleaming marble-and-mahogany luxury of the famous mansion built by John de Koven in 1874, Biggs receives each diner as a guest, and with style, service, and most elegant food, totally recreates for him the state of opulent well-being that the Victorians knew so well how to achieve.

Shrimp in Tomato Aspic
Serves 9 to 10

1 pound shrimp, uncooked
1 carrot, sliced
1 stalk celery and leaves, sliced
1 large onion, sliced
1 bay leaf
6 peppercorns
2 envelopes unflavored gelatin
2 cans (10¾ ounces each) condensed tomato soup
¼ cup dry sherry

Rinse shrimp; place in saucepan; cover with water. Add carrot, celery, onion, bay leaf, and peppercorns. Bring to a boil; simmer about 5 minutes or until tender. Strain ¾ cup cooking liquid; chill. Meanwhile, shell and devein shrimp; cut in pieces. Soften gelatin in cold cooking liquid. Dissolve over low heat; stir in soup and sherry. Chill until slightly thickened. Fold in shrimp. Pour into a single or individual molds.

Veal Scaloppine with Sauce Toscane
Serves 8

1 pair sweetbreads
Boiling salted water

¼ cup butter
2 ripe tomatoes, chopped
2 tablespoons minced onion or shallots
1 can (10½ ounces) condensed chicken broth
1 can (10½ ounces) condensed cream of mushroom soup
1 split bottle champagne
2 tablespoons flour
¼ cup light cream
2 pounds veal scaloppine (Italian style or cut in 8 pieces, pounded very thin)
Salt, pepper, garlic powder
Flour
½ cup butter

Cover sweetbreads with boiling salted water and cook at a simmer until sweetbreads are firm and white. Drain and cool. Remove membranes and gristle and cut sweetbreads into small cubes. Melt ¼ cup butter in a skillet and sauté tomatoes and onions until tomatoes are mushy. Stir in chicken broth, mushroom soup, and champagne. Mix flour and cream. When smooth stir into sauce. Cook until sauce bubbles and thickens, stirring constantly. Fold in sweetbreads. Sprinkle veal with salt, pepper, and garlic powder. Dip slices in flour. Brown veal quickly on both sides in ½ cup hot butter. Spoon sauce over veal. Serve on rice garnished with finely chopped parsley.

Left: Shrimp in Tomato Aspic

Adaptations from recipes by Chef Dennis Michalak.

Beef Tips Basquaise

Serves 6 to 8

4 pounds tenderloin or sirloin tips
Salt, pepper
*½ cup butter or margarine (may use oil or
shortening)*
⅓ cup finely chopped shallots or green onions
½ cup diced green pepper
¼ pound mushrooms, sliced
1 cup red wine
1 can (10½ ounces) condensed beef broth
2 teaspoons Worcestershire sauce
1 can (11 ounces) condensed bisque of tomato soup

If tips are tenderloin they can be cut into thin slices,
sprinkled with salt and pepper and broiled until
medium rare. If the tips are from a tougher cut of
beef they can be roasted or braised until tender, then
thinly sliced.

In a skillet melt butter, add shallots, green pepper,
and mushrooms. Sauté until tender but not brown.
Pour off fat. Add red wine, beef broth and Worcestershire sauce. Bring to a boil and boil gently until liquid
is reduced to half its original volume. Add bisque of
tomato and simmer until sauce thickens slightly.
Spoon sauce over beef tips. Garnish with watercress.

Creamed Vegetables

Serves 6 to 8

*2 packages (10 ounces each) frozen mixed vegetables
(or frozen cauliflower, asparagus, peas,
broccoli, or spinach)
1 can (10¾ ounces) condensed Cheddar
cheese soup
⅓ cup heavy cream*

Cook vegetables according to package directions.
Drain. Add soup and cream to vegetables. Simmer
until bubbly. Serve hot.

Variation: If desired, creamed vegetables may be
poured into a shallow 1-quart casserole and topped
with ½ cup dry bread crumbs mixed with ¼ cup
melted butter. Bake in a preheated 400°F. oven for 15
minutes or until top is lightly browned.

Poitrine de Capon Vieux Carré à la Biggs

Breast of Capon in Cream Sauce
Serves 8

*8 boneless double breasts of capon
2 cups sherry
¼ teaspoon pepper
1 teaspoon salt
2 tablespoons dry mustard
½ cup butter*

Sauce

*½ cup butter
½ cup finely chopped shallots or white onions
¼ cup flour
¼ cup dry mustard
¼ cup paprika
2 tablespoons sherry
1 clove garlic, finely chopped
2 cans (10½ ounces each) condensed chicken broth
2 egg yolks
1 cup heavy cream*

Place chicken breasts in a shallow pan. Combine
sherry, pepper, salt, and dry mustard. Pour over
chicken and let marinate for 1 hour or longer. Drain
and pat dry. Melt ½ cup of butter in a skillet. Brown
chicken breasts on all sides; simmer until chicken is
tender. *For sauce,* melt ½ cup butter, sauté shallots until wilted but not brown. Stir in flour, dry
mustard, paprika, 2 tablespoons sherry, and garlic.
When well blended, gradually blend in chicken broth.
Cook, stirring, until sauce bubbles and thickens. Beat
egg yolks with cream and stir quickly into hot sauce.
Do not boil. Place chicken breasts on a platter and
spoon sauce evenly over them. If desired, chicken can
be garnished with tiny cooked, shelled, and deveined
shrimp and small sautéed mushroom caps. Sprinkle
with chopped parsley.

Poached Fish Cubaine

Serves 4

*4 fish fillets—sole, turbot, flounder
1 shallot, minced
1 carrot, chopped
½ cup chopped celery
1 bay leaf
4 peppercorns
Salt
1 can (10½ ounces) condensed cream of
mushroom soup
¼ pound shrimp—cooked, shelled, deveined
¼ pound crab meat, flaked
⅓ cup heavy cream, whipped*

Place fillets in a shallow pan. Add shallot, carrot,
celery, bay leaf, peppercorns, and sprinkle with salt.
Add just enough water to cover fish. Simmer until fish
turns white and flakes easily. Place fish carefully on a
platter and keep warm. Heat soup and add shrimp
and crab meat. Fold whipped cream into sauce and
reheat just until sauce bubbles. Spoon sauce over fish
fillets. Serve garnished with chopped parsley.

BACCHANAL

Las Vegas, Nevada, is the last place in the world one would go for a quiet, country-type vacation. Las Vegas is a fast-paced gala place, a swinging kind of city. The Bacchanal at Caesars Palace is the kind of restaurant that belongs in Las Vegas. It epitomizes the glitter and excitement of the city and adds a splendor all its own. Exquisite delicacies are prepared by master chefs, served by torch-bearing, toga-clad attendants, with the attractive assistance of "slave girls" and "Oriental maidens."

Mulligatawny Soup

Serves 6

2 leeks, cut into julienne strips
1 small onion, cut into julienne strips
1 small apple, cored, peeled, diced fine
¼ cup butter
¼ teaspoon curry powder
¼ cup flour
2 cans (10½ ounces each) condensed
chicken broth
1 ripe tomato, chopped
2 cups heavy cream
½ cup cooked rice

Sauté leeks, onion, and apple in butter until pale golden brown. Stir in curry powder and flour. Slowly blend in chicken broth; add tomato; stir constantly until smooth and thickened. Simmer slowly 20 minutes. Stir in cream and rice. Reheat but do not boil. Season to taste with salt and pepper.

Germinal Soup

Serves 6 to 8

3 cans (10½ ounces each) condensed chicken broth
3 soup cans water
4 egg yolks

2 cups heavy cream
½ cup sherry
1 cup chopped sorrel or sour grass

Combine chicken broth and water. Heat until simmering. Beat egg yolks and heavy cream; beat in sherry. Sprinkle sorrel into chicken broth. Simmer 5 minutes. Gradually beat egg-yolk mixture into soup. Reheat but do not boil. Season to taste.

Homard à la Crème

Lobster in Cream Sauce
Serves 2 to 3

1 lobster, about 2 pounds, cooked
2 tablespoons butter
Salt, pepper, paprika
1 tablespoon brandy
¼ cup sherry
1 can (10½ ounces) condensed cream of
mushroom soup
¼ cup heavy cream

Remove meat from lobster and dice. Melt butter and sauté lobster. Sprinkle meat with a little salt, pepper, and paprika. Add brandy and warm slightly, set aflame. Stir in sherry. Simmer 5 minutes. Stir in mushroom soup and heavy cream. Simmer only until bubbly. Spoon, if desired, over rice.

Adaptations from recipes by Chef Maurice Gallé.

BLACK BASS HOTEL

Built in 1745, the Black Bass served as a fortified haven for travelers on the Delaware River. In the more than two centuries since that time, the hotel has lived by the motto of those who built it: "Make new friends, keep the old; these are silver, those are gold." The Black Bass is located in Bucks County, Pennsylvania, not far from New Hope, the delightful little town where many artists, writers, and theatrical personalities live and work. The hotel is also near Peddler's Village, a quaint, old-fashioned town filled with little galleries and curio shops and much more for the visitor to enjoy. The Black Bass Hotel overlooks the lovely Delaware and the old Delaware Canal, where visitors may still enjoy an hour-long boat ride on a mule-drawn barge. After such an excursion it is a pleasure to return to the Black Bass for delicious American regional specialties: Bourbon Street Shrimp, for example, or Charleston Meeting Street Crab Meat. There is a branch of the Black Bass restaurant in Manhattan.

Cheese Quiche

Serves 6 to 8

1 unbaked 10-inch pie shell
6 strips bacon, cooked until crisp and crumbled
1 can (10¾ ounces) condensed Cheddar cheese soup
6 egg yolks
Dash Tabasco sauce
6 egg whites, stiffly beaten

The pie shell should have a high fluted edge. Sprinkle crumbled bacon into pie shell. Combine Cheddar cheese soup and egg yolks and beat until well blended. Stir in Tabasco. Fold in beaten egg whites. Pour mixture into pie shell. Bake in a preheated 325°F. oven 40 to 45 minutes, until puffed and golden brown. Serve warm, cut into wedges. Garnish with bacon curls, chopped chives.

Left: Cheese Quiche

Creole Sauce

2 tablespoons butter
1 onion, chopped
1 cup chopped mushrooms
1 clove garlic, chopped
2 tablespoons cognac
1 bay leaf
2 cans (10½ ounces each) condensed
chicken gumbo soup
1½ cups country-style tomato juice
Salt, pepper

Melt butter and sauté onion, mushrooms, and garlic until wilted and golden. Stir in remaining ingredients, seasoning to taste with salt and pepper. Simmer for 10 minutes. Serve mixed with seafood, spooned over rice, noodles, or spaghetti. Use 2 cups of seafood to 1 cup of sauce. Makes about 1 quart of sauce.

Adapted by the late Laurence R. Beines, co-founder.

Baltimore Potted Meat

Serves 6

½ pound salt pork, cut into ¼-inch-thick slices
2 carrots, sliced
½ teaspoon crumbled thyme
1 tablespoon chopped parsley
1 bay leaf
1 pound boneless lean chuck, cut into 1-inch cubes
1 large onion, sliced
1 pound lean boneless pork, cut into 1-inch cubes
¼ cup brandy
1 can (10½ ounces) condensed consommé
2 cloves garlic, chopped
4 mushrooms, chopped
1 cup Burgundy wine
Salt, pepper
3 tablespoons cornstarch mixed with ⅓ cup water

Place in layers, salt pork, carrots, thyme, parsley, bay leaf, chuck, onion, pork, brandy, consommé, garlic, mushrooms, and Burgundy. Cover tightly and place in a preheated 350°F. oven for 3 hours or until meat is tender. Remove from oven. Season to taste with salt and pepper. Slowly stir cornstarch-water mixture into meat and cook, stirring, until sauce bubbles and thickens. Serve hot.

Chilled Curried Soup

Serves 6

2 tablespoons butter
1 tablespoon flour
2 teaspoons curry powder
1 can (10¼ ounces) frozen condensed cream of potato soup
½ cup sour cream
1 cup light cream

In a saucepan melt butter and stir in flour and curry. Add frozen soup, sour cream, and light cream. Cook over low heat, stirring occasionally until soup is smooth and creamy. Cool and then chill. Serve in bowls set into crushed ice. Garnish with finely chopped walnuts and a little freshly grated coconut.

Spicy Barbecue Sauce for Spareribs

Serves 6

1 can (10½ ounces) condensed consommé
1 can (10¾ ounces) condensed tomato soup
2 tablespoons molasses
¼ cup firmly packed dark brown sugar
¼ cup lemon juice
1 teaspoon chili powder
1 teaspoon dry mustard

1 teaspoon crumbled oregano
2 cloves garlic, mashed
2 racks spareribs, about 6 pounds

In a saucepan combine all ingredients except spareribs and simmer for 10 minutes. Roast rib racks in a shallow pan in a preheated 350°F. oven for 1 hour. Drain excess fat. Brush sauce over partially cooked ribs. Continue roasting ribs for 30 to 40 minutes, brushing with sauce every 10 minutes. If barbecuing, partially cook ribs as directed above; place ribs 6 inches above gray coals, brush with sauce and grill for 20 minutes on each side. Brush with sauce every 10 minutes. Makes enough sauce for 2 racks spareribs.

Bourbon Street Shrimp

Serves 6

¼ cup butter
6 mushrooms, sliced
1 can (10 ounces) frozen condensed cream of shrimp soup, thawed
1 cup sour cream
1 teaspoon soy sauce
¼ teaspoon black pepper
1½ pounds shrimp, cooked, shelled, and deveined
Toast slices or cooked rice

Melt butter and sauté mushrooms until wilted but still white. Stir in soup, sour cream, soy sauce, and pepper. Cook, stirring, until sauce bubbles and becomes smooth. Fold in shrimp. Heat until bubbly. Serve spooned over toast slices or cooked rice. Can also be spooned into small casseroles; top each casserole with ⅓ cup grated sharp Cheddar cheese. Place under broiler and broil until bubbly and golden brown.

Charleston Meeting Street Crab Meat

Serves 4

1 can (10 ounces) frozen condensed cream of shrimp soup, thawed
⅓ cup white wine
½ teaspoon Worcestershire sauce
½ cup grated sharp Cheddar cheese
1 pound lump crab meat

In a saucepan combine soup, wine, Worcestershire sauce, and cheese. Heat, stirring, until sauce bubbles and becomes smooth. Fold in crab meat gently and reheat. Serve spooned over rice, toast, or potatoes.

Towns as small as Irwin, Pennsylvania, do not often harbor restaurants of the stature of Ben Gross's. This family-owned establishment has long specialized in excellent baking, fine wines, and a first-class Continental table. Now, in addition, diners in search of the exotic can find it in the Sukoshi Room, where unfamiliar Japanese dishes are prepared and served in authentic style by lovely kimono-clad waitresses.

Ni Ku Dango No O Sui Mono
Meatballs with Vegetable Sauce
Serves 4

½ pound ground pork
¼ pound ground sausage meat (bulk sausage)
1 egg
½ teaspoon salt
½ teaspoon MSG
2 tablespoons cornstarch
3 tablespoons butter
4 new potatoes, diced
3 carrots, diced
2 medium onions, chopped
4 Japanese black mushrooms, diced
3 tablespoons flour
2 cans (10½ ounces each) condensed chicken broth
2 soup cans water
1 cup milk

Mix pork, sausage, egg, salt, MSG, and cornstarch. Shape mixture into bite-size meatballs. Roll meatballs in flour and brown in 1 tablespoon of the butter in a skillet. Remove meatballs. Melt remaining butter and sauté vegetables for 5 minutes. Stir in 3 tablespoons flour. Gradually stir in chicken broth and water. Cook over low heat, stirring constantly, until soup bubbles and thickens slightly. Simmer until vegetables are tender—about 20 minutes. Stir in milk. Add meatballs. Reheat gently, but do not allow the mixture to boil.

Chawan Mushi
Seafood and Chicken with Black Mushrooms
Serves 4

1 flounder fillet, cooked and broken into 8 pieces
2 cups cooked chicken
2 cups cooked deveined shrimp
4 Japanese dried black mushrooms
4 teaspoons soy sauce
4 eggs
1 can (10½ ounces) condensed chicken broth
1 teaspoon sugar
½ teaspoon MSG
1 cup cooked julienne string beans

Divide fish, chicken, shrimp, and mushrooms equally among 4 individual casseroles. Sprinkle casseroles with soy sauce. Beat eggs with chicken broth, sugar, and MSG. Pour ¼ of the mixture over each casserole. Cover and place casseroles in a pan holding 1 inch of water. Bake in a preheated 350°F. oven for 25 minutes. Serve topped with hot string beans.

Adaptations from recipes by Chef Robert Lilley.

THE BLUE HORSE

The capital of Minnesota, St. Paul, began as a small settlement at the confluence of the Mississippi and Minnesota Rivers, rejoicing in the odd name of Pig's Eye. It became the site of Fort Snelling, once the farthest northwest outpost of the United States. The fort's handsome round tower is now a museum. Also worth seeing are the Capitol Building, which boasts the largest unsupported marble dome in the world, and the City Hall and Court House, which are furnished in rare woods. After sight-seeing, dinner at The Blue Horse can be an event, for the restaurant has won many awards and recommendations from gourmet societies. The restaurant takes its name from the focal point of its décor: a massive beaten copper relief of a stallion. The menu shows a strong West Coast influence—such specialties as Scalloped Olympia Oysters and Dungeness Crab Cheddar—for the owner, Clifford Warling, spent some years in the restaurant business in the West before returning to St. Paul.

Scalloped Olympia Oysters
Serves 6

2 cans (10 ounces each) frozen condensed oyster
stew, thawed
1 quart shucked drained Olympia oysters
(or regular-size oysters)
¼ cup flour
¾ cup coarsely crushed crackers
6 tablespoons butter
Paprika

Drain liquid from oyster stew and reserve. Mix oysters from stew with fresh oysters. Place oysters in 6 individual casseroles. Stir drained oyster stew into flour gradually. Cook over low heat, stirring constantly, until mixture bubbles and thickens. Simmer 5 minutes. Spoon hot sauce over oysters. Sprinkle tops of casseroles with cracker crumbs. Dot with butter. Bake in a preheated 400°F. oven 15 minutes or until bubbly and browned. Sprinkle with paprika.

Left: Scalloped Olympia Oysters

Dungeness Crab Cheddar
Serves 4

1 pound shelled Dungeness crab meat or 2 cans
(7¾ ounces each) king crab meat or 1
pound lump crab meat
¼ cup butter
½ cup white wine
4 English muffins, split and toasted
1 can (10¾ ounces) condensed Cheddar cheese soup
2 drops Tabasco sauce
Sprinkle cayenne
⅓ cup light cream

Sauté crab meat in butter until hot. Add white wine and simmer 5 minutes. Place English muffins in a shallow pan. Spoon crab meat on muffins. Combine remaining ingredients and heat until bubbly. Spoon sauce over crab meat. Place under broiler and broil until golden brown. Serve garnished with parsley and pitted black olives.

Adapted by Owner Clifford Warling.

Roast Grouse with Wild Rice

Serves 4

2 grouse, about 1½ pounds each
Salt
½ cup chopped onion
½ cup chopped mushrooms
1 can (10½ ounces) condensed consommé
⅛ teaspoon crumbled oregano
1 cup wild rice
Water
1 medium onion, chopped
2 carrots, chopped
1 apple, peeled and chopped
1 can (10½ ounces) condensed cream of
mushroom soup
¼ cup light cream
¼ cup red wine

Rub grouse inside and out with salt. Combine onions, mushrooms, consommé, oregano, and wild rice. Bring to a boil and simmer until rice is tender, about 40 to 45 minutes, adding water when necessary to keep rice from sticking. When rice is tender, season to taste with salt. Stuff grouse with rice. Place onion, carrots, and apple in a shallow roasting pan and place grouse on top, breast side down. Roast in a preheated 350°F. oven for 30 minutes. Turn grouse breast side up and roast until brown and tender, about 1½ to 2 hours. Remove grouse to a platter and keep warm. Strain pan juices into a saucepan. Stir in soup, cream, and wine. Simmer, stirring, until sauce bubbles. Spoon sauce over grouse. Garnish with additional cooked wild rice.

Sauce Bordelaise Wandzel

4 marrow bones, about 2 inches long
2 tablespoons butter
2 tablespoons flour
1 can (10½ ounces) condensed beef broth
¼ cup "V-8" juice
2 tablespoons concentrated beef extract
½ teaspoon sugar
½ cup red wine
1 tablespoon finely chopped shallots or white onion

Cover bones with water and boil until marrow is easily removed from bones. Remove marrow and mash. Combine mashed marrow and butter in a saucepan. Stir in flour. Gradually stir in beef broth, "V-8", beef extract, sugar, red wine, and shallots. Cook over low heat, stirring constantly, until sauce bubbles and thickens. Spoon over broiled slices of beef filet, slices of roast beef, or broiled steak. Makes about 2 cups of sauce.

Brussels Sprouts Cheddar

Serves 6 to 8

2 pounds Brussels sprouts
1 can (10¾ ounces) condensed
Cheddar cheese soup
Dash Worcestershire sauce
2 drops Tabasco sauce
Dash cayenne pepper
Paprika

Wash and trim Brussels sprouts. Cut sprouts into halves and cook in boiling salted water to cover until sprouts are tender but still firm and slightly crisp. Combine soup, Worcestershire sauce, Tabasco, and cayenne. Place well-drained sprouts in a shallow baking dish. Spoon soup mixture over sprouts. Sprinkle with paprika. Place under broiler until lightly browned.

Pork Chops à la Jenni

Serves 6

12 to 18 center-cut pork chops, sliced
¼ inch thick
Salt, pepper
Flour
½ cup butter
1 can (10½ ounces) condensed cream of
mushroom soup
½ cup grated Parmesan cheese
Paprika

Season pork chops with salt and pepper. Dip chops into flour and shake off excess. Brown chops on both sides in butter in a large skillet. Place chops in overlapping rows in a shallow casserole. Spoon pan drippings over chops. Spread mushroom soup over chops. Sprinkle with Parmesan cheese and paprika. Bake covered in a preheated 350°F. oven 15 to 20 minutes.

Baked Ham and Asparagus Roll with Cheddar Cheese Sauce

Serves 4

24 fresh, frozen, or canned asparagus spears
8 slices boiled ham, 4 x 6 inches
2 cans (10¾ ounces each) condensed Cheddar
cheese soup
¼ teaspoon paprika
2 teaspoons prepared mustard
⅓ cup light cream

Place 3 asparagus spears at the end of each slice of ham. Roll up and place rolls side by side in a shallow casserole. Combine remaining ingredients; blend well, spoon over asparagus. Bake in preheated 350°F. oven 30 minutes. Serve with hash browned potatoes.

CAFÉ JOHNELL

French is spoken by the food at the Café Johnell, in Fort Wayne, Indiana. And the discriminating diner can enjoy it in three very Gallic settings: in the plush red-velvet booths of La Galerie, at the smaller tables of the Petite Allée, or beneath the glittering chandeliers on the gold love seats of splendid La Chambre. The Café Johnell also rejoices in one of the finest wine cellars in the country, which has been decorated with the coveted award of Le Grand Conseil de l'Académie des Vins de Bordeaux. Dining and wining at Café Johnell is like a visit to Paris at its glamorous best.

King Crab Bisque

Serves 4 to 6

1 can (11¼ ounces) condensed green pea soup
1 can (10¾ ounces) condensed tomato soup
1 soup can light cream
1 soup can milk
2 cups flaked cooked crab
½ cup bourbon
Chopped parsley

Blend soups until smooth. Gradually stir in cream and milk; add crab. Heat, stirring often. Do not boil. Add bourbon. Reheat; garnish with parsley.

Mustard Sauce

½ cup butter
¼ cup flour
1 cup dry white wine
1 can (10½ ounces) condensed beef broth
2 tablespoons Dijon mustard
Salt

Melt butter in a saucepan and stir in flour. Gradually stir in wine and beef broth. Add mustard and stir over low heat until sauce bubbles and thickens. Season to taste. Serve with boiled beef, broiled fish, lamb chops, or veal. Makes about 2¼ cups of sauce.

Mushrooms Bordelaise

Serves 4

1 cup red wine
¼ cup chopped shallots or white onions
Dash of black pepper
Dash of crumbled thyme
½ bay leaf
1 can (10½ ounces) condensed beef broth
¼ cup flour mixed with ½ cup water
1 pound small button mushrooms
¼ cup butter
Buttered toast slices

In a saucepan combine red wine, shallots, pepper, thyme, bay leaf, and beef broth. Simmer for 15 minutes. Stir in flour mixture and continue stirring over low heat until sauce bubbles and thickens. Sauté mushrooms in butter until golden brown and cooked. Remove bay leaf from sauce; fold in mushrooms. Serve over thin slices of well-buttered toast.

Adapted by Owner-Chef John Spillson.

CHEZ LOUIS

Scottsdale, a prosperous residential suburb of Phoenix, Arizona, as well as a popular resort, is in part a reconstruction of an old Western town. Here Louis Germain, seeking escape from the hurry and noise of big cities, opened his restaurant, Chez Louis. Although the building is unpretentious, on a street lined with hitching posts and bumper logs, the food is superb and the atmosphere is delightfully restful and attractive. The menu is largely French, with most entrées prepared to order. Chez Louis is open year round in Scottsdale, and in the summer season in Durango, Colorado.

Tripes à la Mode de Caen

Serves 4

1½ pounds tripe
¼ cup butter
1 tablespoon oil
2 carrots, chopped
2 cloves garlic, chopped
2 onions, chopped
2 strips bacon, chopped
2 tablespoons chopped parsley
Pinch thyme
Pinch cayenne
1 calf's foot
1 cup white wine
2 cans (10½ ounces each) condensed chicken broth
1 cup water

Cover tripe with water and simmer for 1 hour. Drain and cut into 2-inch squares. Melt butter, add oil; sauté carrots, garlic, onions, and bacon until tender. Pour vegetables and drippings into a 1½-quart casserole with a tight-fitting lid. Add tripe and remaining ingredients. Cover tightly and bake in a preheated 300°F. oven for 7 to 8 hours, or until tripe is very tender. Remove calf's foot and skim off excess grease. If lid does not fit tightly it may be necessary to add water from time to time to prevent sticking. A bean pot is excellent for cooking this dish. Serve very hot.

Squab Rembouiller

Serves 4

4 squab
Salt, pepper
¼ cup butter
2 shallots, minced, or 2 tablespoons minced white onion
⅓ cup country-style tomato juice
½ cup dry white wine
1 can (10½ ounces) condensed cream of mushroom soup
¼ cup finely chopped parsley

Sprinkle squab inside and out with salt and pepper. Melt butter; brown birds on all sides. Remove squab; sauté shallots until golden. Replace squab and add remaining ingredients. Cover tightly; simmer for 40 minutes or until squab are tender. Serve with pan juices spooned over squab.

Adaptations from recipes by Owner-Chef Louis Germain.

Croûte of Mushrooms

Serves 6

2 tablespoons butter
2 tablespoons chopped onion
1 pound fresh mushrooms, sliced
1 can (10½ ounces) condensed cream of chicken soup
¼ cup white wine
1 tablespoon lemon juice
6 toast slices

Melt butter and sauté onion until golden. Add mushrooms and sauté until wilted. Stir in soup, wine, and lemon juice. Cook until bubbly, then simmer 10 minutes. Spoon hot over toast slices.

Eggs Florentine

Serves 4

2 packages (10 ounces each) frozen chopped spinach
1 teaspoon salt
¼ teaspoon pepper
⅛ teaspoon garlic powder
8 poached eggs
1 can (10¾ ounces) condensed
Cheddar cheese soup
½ cup heavy cream

Prepare chopped spinach as directed on package. Drain well, pressing out all excess moisture. Mix spinach with salt, pepper, and garlic powder. Spoon mixture into 4 individual casseroles. Top spinach with hot poached eggs. Combine Cheddar cheese soup and cream. Heat until bubbly and spoon over poached eggs. Serve at once.

Riz de Veau à l'Ancienne

Sweetbreads and Kidneys, Old Style
Serves 4

2 pairs sweetbreads
1 can (10½ ounces) condensed chicken broth
2 tablespoons butter
4 lamb kidneys, trimmed and diced into
½-inch cubes
1 can (⅞ ounce) truffles, finely chopped
1 cup chopped fresh mushrooms
¼ cup heavy cream
¼ cup Madeira wine
1 can (10½ ounces) condensed cream of chicken soup
Salt

In a saucepan combine sweetbreads and chicken broth. Simmer until sweetbreads have turned white and firm. Drain and discard broth. Remove skin and trimmings from sweetbreads. Cut sweetbreads into thick slices

and place in a serving dish. Cover and keep warm. In a skillet, heat butter. Add lamb kidneys, half of the truffles, and the mushrooms. Sauté until kidneys are just cooked. Stir in cream, Madeira, and chicken soup. Simmer for 10 minutes. Season to taste with salt. Spoon hot sauce over sweetbread slices; sprinkle with remaining truffles.

Fennel Braisé

Serves 4

1 strip bacon, chopped
¼ cup marrow (4 pieces marrow bone, about 2 inches long)
1 can (10½ ounces) condensed onion soup
1 carrot, chopped
1 tablespoon chopped parsley
2 bunches fennel, trimmed and cut into 4-inch strips
Salt, pepper

Combine bacon, marrow, onion soup, carrot, and parsley in a large saucepan. Bring to a boil, lower heat and simmer. Trim fennel until only green stalks and white stalks remain. Add fennel to simmering broth. Toss to coat, cover tightly and simmer for 15 minutes or until fennel is tender crisp. Season to taste.

Quail Chasseur

Serves 4

4 quail
Salt, pepper
¼ cup butter
2 tablespoons flour
1 can (10½ ounces) condensed consommé
Pinch thyme
½ bay leaf
½ cup white wine

Sprinkle quail inside and out with salt and pepper. Melt butter in a skillet and brown quail on all sides slowly over medium heat. Sprinkle quail with flour. Add remaining ingredients; cover tightly and simmer for 40 minutes or until quail are tender. Serve quail with some of the pan juices spooned over them.

Brennan's

New Orleans is for jazz, for the romantic balconies and twisting byways of the French Quarter—and for world-renowned restaurants like Brennan's. Despite its Irish name, Brennan's serves extraordinary French-Creole food and something very hard to come by even among the greatest restaurants: fabulous breakfasts. There are also Brennan's restaurants, serving the same superb cuisine, in Houston and Dallas, Texas.

Tournedos Royale

Filets of Beef with Stuffed Artichoke Bottoms
Serves 4

¼ cup butter
½ cup chopped onion
⅓ cup dry bread crumbs
1 teaspoon paprika
1 teaspoon capers
1 teaspoon minced truffles
Pinch thyme
½ cup finely chopped cooked sweetbreads
4 canned artichoke bottoms
4 filets mignons, 10 ounces each
Garlic
Salt, pepper

Heat butter and sauté onion until tender and golden. Add bread crumbs, paprika, capers, truffles, thyme, and sweetbreads. Cool. Shape mixture into 4 balls. Place 1 ball in each artichoke bottom. Rub filets with garlic and sprinkle with salt and pepper. Broil to doneness desired. Top with stuffed artichoke bottom. Spoon Béarnaise Sauce (page 36) over stuffed artichoke bottoms and filets mignons.

Left: Tournedos Royale

Consommé Shaw

Serves 8

1 large onion, minced
1 cup minced celery
1 carrot, minced
1 cup canned tomatoes, chopped
3 egg whites and the shells of 3 eggs
2 teaspoons white pepper
Pinch cayenne
3 cans (10½ ounces each) condensed beef broth
3 soup cans water
3 bottles (8 ounces each) clam juice

Combine all ingredients except clam juice and simmer, covered, for 1½ hours. Remove from heat and strain through several thicknesses of cheesecloth. Stir in clam juice and reheat. Garnish with finely chopped parsley.

Jellied Consommé with Sour Cream

Omit clam juice. Soak 2 tablespoons unflavored gelatin in ¼ cup water for 5 minutes. Stir into hot strained consommé until dissolved. Chill until firm. Beat with a fork and spoon into soup cups. Garnish each cup with sour cream.

Adaptations from recipes by Chef Paul Blange.

Béarnaise Sauce

1 clove garlic, mashed
Salt, pepper
1 can (10½ ounces) cream of chicken soup
¼ cup melted butter
1 to 3 teaspoons lemon juice
1 to 3 teaspoons tarragon vinegar
2 tablespoons drained capers
¼ cup finely chopped parsley

Combine all ingredients and heat until bubbly.

Marinated Venison

Serves 6

1 venison roast, about 4 pounds
1 teaspoon cracked pepper
3 bay leaves
½ teaspoon ground allspice
6 whole cloves
½ cup brandy
½ cup Burgundy wine
½ cup oil
6 carrots, cut into 2-inch lengths
12 small white onions, peeled, left whole
¼ cup butter
¼ cup flour
1 can (10½ ounces) condensed beef broth
Salt

Place venison roast in an earthenware or glass bowl. Add pepper, bay leaves, allspice, cloves, brandy, Burgundy, and oil. Cover and refrigerate overnight. Drain

roast and place in a shallow roasting pan. Pour marinade into bottom of pan. Roast in a preheated 350°F. oven for 2 to 2½ hours or until venison is tender. Spoon marinade over meat every 15 to 20 minutes. Add carrots and onions to roast 40 minutes before roast is ready. Remove cooked meat and vegetables to a platter and keep warm. Measure 1 cup of the pan drippings. In a saucepan melt butter and stir in flour. Gradually stir in pan drippings, beef broth. Cook over low heat, stirring constantly, until sauce bubbles and thickens. Season to taste with salt. Slice meat, serve with vegetables. Spoon sauce over meat.

Turtle Soup au Sherry

Serves 8

1 can (2 pounds 1 ounce) green turtle meat
½ cup butter
1½ cups chopped white onions
½ cup flour
1 can (10¾ ounces) condensed tomato soup
½ cup sherry
¼ cup Worcestershire sauce
2 eggs, hard-cooked and finely chopped
½ cup finely chopped parsley
½ lemon, thinly sliced

Drain turtle meat and reserve liquid. Add enough water to liquid to make 5 cups. Dice turtle meat into ½-inch cubes. In a large kettle, melt butter and sauté onions until transparent but not brown. Stir in flour and cook until flour turns pale golden brown. Stir in tomato soup, turtle liquid, sherry, and Worcestershire sauce. Let simmer, stirring occasionally, for 15 minutes. Add eggs, parsley, lemon slices, and turtle meat. Simmer another 15 minutes. Serve at once. If desired, serve with extra sherry at the table. Spoon 1 or 2 tablespoons sherry into each serving and stir lightly.

Vichyssoise
Potato Soup
Serves 6 to 8

1 onion, sliced
½ cup minced celery
1 cup diced smoked ham
Water
2 cans (10½ ounces each) condensed cream
of potato soup
1½ cups milk
1½ cups light cream
1 tablespoon Worcestershire sauce
Cayenne, salt

In a large saucepan combine onion, celery, and ham. Add water to cover. Simmer, covered, until vegetables are tender. Press mixture through a sieve or whirl in a blender. Return to saucepan and add remaining ingredients. Season to taste with cayenne and salt. Heat until soup starts to bubble. Serve hot or icy cold, sprinkled with finely chopped scallions, or chives.

Eggs Nouvelle Orléans

Serves 4

½ cup butter
1 pound fresh lump crab meat
Salt, pepper
8 eggs
2 tablespoons white vinegar
1 can (10½ ounces) condensed cream of potato
soup, sieved
⅓ cup light cream
2 tablespoons brandy

Melt butter in a skillet and sauté crab meat for 5 minutes. Season to taste with salt and pepper. Poach eggs in water with 2 tablespoons white vinegar added. Spoon crab meat into 4 individual shallow casseroles. Top each casserole with 2 poached eggs. In a saucepan combine potato soup, cream, and brandy. Cook, stirring, until bubbly. Spoon hot sauce over eggs. Serve immediately with toast or garlic bread.

Eggs St. Denis

Serves 4

8 Holland rusks
8 slices boiled or smoked ham sautéed in
¼ cup butter
8 poached eggs
Marchand de Vin Sauce

Put rusks on a plate (2 to each serving) and place ham across both. Place poached eggs on ham. Spoon hot sauce over eggs. Serve at once.

Marchand de Vin Sauce

¾ cup butter
⅓ cup finely chopped mushrooms
½ cup minced ham, smoked or boiled
⅓ cup minced shallots or white onions
½ cup finely chopped yellow onions
2 tablespoons minced garlic
2 tablespoons flour
1 can (10½ ounces) condensed beef broth
Dash cayenne
½ cup red wine
Salt, pepper

Melt butter and sauté mushrooms, ham, shallots, onions, and garlic until golden. Stir in flour. Gradually stir in beef broth, cayenne, and wine. Cook over low heat, stirring constantly, until sauce bubbles and thickens. Season to taste with salt and pepper. Makes 2 cups of sauce.

Quail in White Wine

Serves 4

4 quail, about ¾ pound each
¾ cup melted butter
Salt, pepper
3 tablespoons flour
1 can (10½ ounces) condensed chicken broth
¾ cup water
½ cup Sauternes
Dash cayenne

Split quail down center breast and open flat. Brush lightly with some of the melted butter. Sprinkle on both sides with salt and pepper. Broil quail 15 to 20 minutes or until golden brown on both sides. Pour remaining butter into a skillet. Stir in flour. Gradually stir in chicken broth, water, and Sauternes. Cook over low heat, stirring constantly, until sauce bubbles and thickens. Add cayenne and broiled quail. Simmer, covered, 15 to 20 minutes or until quail are tender.

Duck Jambalaya

Serves 4

1 cup flour
1 teaspoon salt
¼ teaspoon cayenne
1 duckling, about 3½ pounds, cut up
¼ cup butter
1 cup finely chopped white onions
1 cup finely chopped green onions
2 cans (10½ ounces each) condensed chicken broth
1½ cups water
2 cups converted raw rice

Combine flour with salt and cayenne. Roll pieces of duckling in mixture. Brown duckling in butter in a Dutch oven. Add white and green onion and sauté until onion is wilted. Add chicken broth and water and simmer for 35 minutes, covered. Add rice and simmer, covered, for another 30 minutes, or until rice is tender. Add more water, if necessary, to keep rice from sticking. Serve hot, garnished with chopped parsley.

Cape Cod Room

Homesick Cape Codders can come to grateful rest in the Cape Cod Room of Chicago's Drake Hotel, a haven so salty it might be anywhere between Falmouth and Provincetown. Here, as the seafood buff relishes exceptional specialties of the house, he can pretend for a while that the sea fog is lowering outside and that the Atlantic is something less than fifteen hundred miles away. One charming feature of the Cape Cod Room is a sea captain's stove, with the missing captain's coat and hat beside it.

Pompano en Papillote

Serves 6

6 pompano fillets
1 cup rosé wine
¼ cup butter
½ cup finely chopped mushrooms
1 tablespoon minced shallots or white onions
1 can (11 ounces) condensed bisque of tomato soup
1½ cups diced cooked fresh or canned lobster

Place pompano fillets in a shallow skillet. Add wine, butter, mushrooms, and shallots. Cover tightly and simmer over low heat until fish flakes, about 15 minutes. Drain and remove fish and place on 6 12-inch squares of parchment paper. (Heavy duty aluminum foil may be substituted.) Boil liquid remaining in skillet until liquid is almost absorbed. Stir in tomato bisque. Top pompano with lobster pieces. Divide sauce equally among pieces of fish. Seal packets tightly. Bake on a cookie sheet in a preheated 400°F. oven for 15 minutes or until packets puff. These foil packets can be prepared ahead of time and refrigerated until needed. Allow 5 minutes' extra baking time if packets have been refrigerated.

Left: Pompano en Papillote

Red Snapper Soup

Serves 4

1 red snapper, about 2 to 2½ pounds, cleaned
and scaled
2½ cups water
1 tablespoon whole pickling spice
1 teaspoon salt
2 tablespoons butter
¼ cup diced onion
½ cup diced celery
½ cup diced green pepper
1 can (10½ ounces) condensed beef broth
1 can (10¾ ounces) condensed tomato soup
½ cup sherry

Place whole fish in a large skillet. Add water, pickling spice, and salt. Cover and simmer for 10 to 15 minutes or until fish is easily flaked. Strain broth and reserve 2 cups. Melt butter in a large kettle and brown onion, celery, and green pepper. Add fish stock and simmer gently until vegetables are tender. Stir in beef broth and tomato soup. Bone and skin fish and break into large chunks. Add fish to soup. Stir in wine and simmer for 5 minutes. Serve hot, sprinkled with finely chopped fresh dill.

Adaptations from recipes by Chef John Kaufmann.

Cellar

If proof were needed that time is running faster and the world is getting smaller, Oklahoma City is ready to provide it. For here, in a place that only a few decades ago held little but oil and Indians and qualified as a part of the Wild West, in a city whose name is synonymous with the purely American dream, one finds the Cellar—very Continental, so thoroughly French in spirit and in cuisine that it would be quite at home under the lovely chestnut trees of Paris, with the Seine providing the background.

Perdrix Vallée d'Auge
Partridge with Apple Wedges
Serves 4

4 partridges, about ¾ pound each, split
Salt, pepper
⅓ cup butter
2 tablespoons oil
⅓ cup Calvados, applejack, or cider
1 can (10½ ounces) condensed cream of
chicken soup
4 tart apples, cored and cut into wedges
¼ cup butter
¼ cup firmly packed brown sugar
1 teaspoon lemon juice

Sprinkle partridge halves with salt and pepper. Heat the ⅓ cup butter and oil in a large skillet. Brown partridges on all sides. Lower heat, cover and simmer for 25 minutes or until partridges are tender. Add Calvados and set aflame. When flames die stir in soup. Sauté the apple wedges in the ¼ cup butter until they are tender but still firm. Sprinkle them with brown sugar and lemon juice and toss to blend. To serve, spoon Calvados sauce onto a platter and place partridges on top of sauce. Decorate with apple wedges.

Left: Perdrix Vallée d'Auge

Sauce Aurore

1 can (10¾ ounces) condensed tomato soup
¼ cup heavy cream
1 tablespoon chopped parsley
1 tablespoon chopped chives
1 teaspoon Worcestershire sauce
1 tablespoon Madeira wine

Combine all ingredients in a saucepan and simmer until bubbly. Spoon over meat loaf, veal chops, omelettes, chicken soufflé. Makes about 1½ cups of sauce.

Poached Eggs with Asparagus Sauce
Serves 6

6 artichoke bottoms, sautéed in butter
6 poached eggs
Salt, pepper
1 can (10½ ounces) condensed cream of
asparagus soup
½ teaspoon Worcestershire sauce
2 drops Tabasco sauce
2 tablespoons lemon juice
¼ cup dry sherry
2 tablespoons melted butter

Place hot artichoke bottoms on a platter and top with poached eggs. Sprinkle eggs with salt and pepper. Combine remaining ingredients and simmer until bubbly. Spoon hot sauce over poached eggs. Serve at once.

Adapted by Chef John Bennett.

Poached Trout Duxelles

Serves 4

4 trout
Salt, pepper
1 can (10½ ounces) condensed chicken broth
Water
1 pound finely chopped fresh mushrooms
¼ cup butter
¼ cup minced shallots or white onions
1 tablespoon chopped parsley
½ teaspoon salt
¼ teaspoon pepper
2 teaspoons lemon juice
1 can (10 ounces) frozen condensed cream of
shrimp soup, thawed
¼ cup light cream
1 egg yolk
1 tablespoon cognac
2 tablespoons lemon juice
¼ cup heavy cream, whipped

Thaw trout if frozen, wash and pat dry. Sprinkle trout with salt and pepper. Place trout in a shallow pan. Add chicken broth and enough water to cover the trout. Bring to a boil; lower heat and simmer for 15 to 20 minutes or until trout are cooked. Remove head, tail, and skin from trout. Sauté mushrooms in butter. Add shallots and sauté until vegetables are tender. Add parsley, salt, pepper, and lemon juice. Spoon mixture onto a shallow heatproof platter, spreading it evenly. Place trout on top. In saucepan, combine shrimp soup, cream, egg yolk, cognac, lemon juice. Heat, stirring, to boiling point. *Do not boil.* Fold in whipped cream. Spoon evenly over trout. Broil till sauce glazes.

Eminçe of Veal

Serves 4

6 tablespoons butter
¾ cup minced onion
1 clove garlic, minced
1 pound very thin Italian-style veal cutlets, cut into
½-inch strips
1 can (10½ ounces) condensed cream of
mushroom soup

1 tablespoon lemon juice
½ teaspoon crumbled tarragon
2 tablespoons Madeira wine

Melt butter in a skillet; sauté onion and garlic until tender but not brown. Add veal strips and continue cooking until meat is tender. This will take only a few minutes. Stir in remaining ingredients and simmer for 5 minutes. Serve with rice pilaf.

Carrots in Cream and Dill

Serves 6

1 bunch carrots
1 cup sliced onions
1 clove garlic, minced
¼ cup olive oil
1 tablespoon flour
1 can (10½ ounces) condensed cream of
celery soup
1 cup milk
½ teaspoon dill seed or 1 tablespoon
chopped dill
1 teaspoon sugar
Salt, pepper, allspice

Scrape carrots and cut into julienne strips. Sauté carrots, onions, and garlic in oil for 5 minutes. Sprinkle with flour. Stir in soup and milk. Add dill and sugar. Simmer until carrots are tender, about 25 to 30 minutes, stirring occasionally. Season to taste with salt, pepper, and allspice.

Overtones of Provence and New Orleans color the charming provincial setting of Danny's in Baltimore. This is a family-run restaurant, but the food it serves could never emerge from a family kitchen unless it was run by a dynasty of *cordons bleus*. An excellent wine list supports a choice of specialties that derive from the finest cooking of many nations, superbly interpreted in Danny's kitchen. Many of the soups and sauces served at Danny's are the special creations of Chef Danny Dickman himself.

Creamed Spinach

Serves 4 to 6

*2 pounds fresh spinach or 2 packages (10 ounces
each) frozen chopped spinach
1 can (10½ ounces) condensed cream of celery soup
⅓ cup light cream
Dash nutmeg*

Wash spinach in several changes of water to remove all sand. Place in a large kettle with a small amount of water and cook covered until spinach is wilted and just tender. Drain, pressing out all liquid, then chop. (When using frozen spinach cook as directed on package, and press out all liquid.) Combine spinach, soup, cream, and nutmeg in a saucepan. Heat until mixture bubbles.

Tournedos Rossini with Madeira Mushroom Sauce

Serves 6

*6 filets mignons, 1 inch thick
½ cup butter
Salt, pepper
6 slices toast, trimmed to fit meat
1 can (4¾ ounces) pâté de foie gras, cut into
6 slices
1 truffle, cut into 6 slices*

*6 large mushroom caps sautéed in butter
Madeira Mushroom Sauce*

Brown filets in butter until the desired degree of doneness. Season to taste with salt and pepper. Place each tournedo on toast slice and top with slice of pâté and slice of truffle. Top with mushroom cap. Spoon hot Madeira Mushroom Sauce over tournedos and serve garnished with watercress.

Madeira Mushroom Sauce

*½ pound mushrooms, sliced
1 tablespoon butter
2 tablespoons flour
1 tablespoon minced shallots or white onions
1 can (10½ ounces) condensed beef broth
¼ cup Madeira wine
¼ cup sherry
1 teaspoon minced parsley
Salt, pepper*

Sauté mushrooms in butter. Sprinkle with flour and onions. Gradually stir in beef broth, Madeira, and sherry. Cook, stirring, until sauce bubbles and thickens. Add parsley, salt, and pepper to taste. Makes 2 cups, about 6 servings.

Adaptations from recipes by Owner-Chef Danny Dickman.

ERNIE'S

Soaring hills, the wind from the sea, a sense of adventure—for a dozen reasons, San Francisco is one of the most exciting cities in the world. And among its charms is Ernie's, whose rich turn-of-the-century ambience and superlative food have made this San Francisco landmark a gourmet's mecca of international reputation.

Saddle of Lamb Marie Louise

Serves 6

1 saddle of lamb, 4 to 5 pounds (7 to 8 pounds,
untrimmed)
Salt, pepper, crumbled thyme, bay leaf, tarragon
1 onion, chopped
1 cup Marsala wine
1 can (10½ ounces) condensed beef broth
1 can (10¾ ounces) condensed tomato soup
2 packages (9 ounces each) frozen artichoke hearts
1 cup button mushrooms, stems removed
12 small new potatoes, cooked
¾ cup butter or margarine
3 tomatoes, cut into halves
¼ cup grated Parmesan cheese
1 can (20 ounces) celery hearts
(coeurs de céleri)

Trim saddle of lamb, removing skin, fat, and kidneys. Sprinkle meat with salt and pepper. Rub meat with crumbled herbs. Shape meat into a round piece and roast in a shallow pan on a rack in a preheated 450°F. oven for 35 to 40 minutes (lamb will be pink in the French manner). Remove lamb to a platter and keep warm. Drain excess fat from roasting pan. Add onion, Marsala, and beef broth to pan. Cook on top of range, scraping all particles. Bring to a boil and boil gently until liquid is half its original volume. Stir in tomato soup. Simmer until sauce is thickened. Sauté thawed artichoke hearts, mushrooms, potatoes in ½ cup of the butter until golden. Sprinkle tomatoes with salt and pepper. Dot with remaining butter and broil until tomatoes are easily pierced. In small pan, heat celery hearts in broth from can. Drain, sprinkle with grated Parmesan cheese. Serve lamb on a platter surrounded by artichoke hearts, button mushrooms, potatoes, tomatoes, celery hearts. Garnish with parsley.

Grenadine of Beef Tenderloin

Serves 8

8 slices filet mignon, 1 inch thick
8 long strips sliced bacon, ½ inch wide
Salt, pepper
⅓ cup butter
16 small mushrooms
1½ cups Sauce Chasseur (see index)
1 cup Sauce Béarnaise (see index)

Pound beef until like scaloppini. Using a larding needle insert 1 strip of bacon in each piece of beef. Sprinkle meat on both sides with salt and pepper. Melt butter and sauté beef until the desired degree of doneness. Add mushrooms and sauté until golden brown. Heat Sauce Chasseur and spoon onto a platter. Top with beef slices and mushrooms. Spread meat with Sauce Béarnaise and place under broiler for 1 minute. Serve at once.

Left: Saddle of Lamb Marie Louise

Adaptations from recipes by Co-Owner Roland Gotti.

Médaillons Helder
Filets of Beef with Marsala Sauce
Serves 4

4 filets mignons, 1 inch thick
Salt, pepper
¼ cup butter
½ cup Marsala wine
1 cup Brown Sauce (strained without pressing
vegetables through sieve)
¾ cup Béarnaise Sauce (see index)
2 tomatoes, chopped and sautéed in 2 tablespoons
butter and seasoned with salt
2 tablespoons finely chopped truffles
4 slices bread, crusts trimmed and cut into
triangles
¼ cup oil

Season filets with salt and pepper. Melt butter and
sauté filets about 4 minutes on each side. Remove
filets and add Marsala and Brown Sauce to pan drippings. Simmer 2 to 3 minutes, scraping pan. Replace
filets in sauce and spread ½ cup of the Béarnaise
Sauce over tops of filets. Spoon hot tomatoes over
Béarnaise Sauce. Sprinkle with truffles. Simmer 10
minutes. Sauté bread triangles in oil until golden
brown on both sides. Place filets on a platter and surround with bread triangles. Beat remaining Béarnaise
Sauce into sauce in pan. Serve this sauce with the filets.
Garnish the médaillons with a nest of julienne potatoes, glazed carrots, artichoke bottoms stuffed with
creamed button mushrooms, and glazed half tomatoes
filled with spinach purée.

Tenderloin en Brochette
Serves 8

8 slices filet mignon, 1 inch thick
4 green peppers
½ pound thick-sliced bacon
Salt, pepper, olive oil

Cut meat into 2-inch squares; cut green peppers into
1½-inch squares; cut bacon into 2-inch pieces. Alternate filet, pepper, and bacon on skewers. Sprinkle
with salt and pepper. Brush with olive oil. Broil to desired degree of doneness. Serve with Sauce Chasseur.

Brown Sauce
(a base for other sauces)

2 pounds veal-shank bones
2 large onions, coarsely chopped
2 carrots, scraped and chopped
1 cup chopped celery

2 tablespoons flour
2 cans (10½ ounces each) condensed consommé
1 can (12 ounces) "V-8" juice
2 quarts water

Preheat oven to 500°F. Place bones in a 6-quart
Dutch oven or other casserole. Brown bones for 20
minutes. Add onions, carrots, and celery and brown
another 10 minutes. Sprinkle with flour and brown
another 10 minutes. Add consommé,"V-8" and water.
Replace in oven and continue cooking until stock
begins to boil. Lower heat to 400°F. and cook for 1½
hours. Remove from oven and let cool. Remove bones.
Strain broth and then chill. When cold take off the
top layer of fat. Discard and use broth underneath as
a base for any sauce requiring Brown Sauce. Makes
about 1 quart of sauce.

Sauce Chasseur

½ pound small mushrooms, sliced
1 tablespoon butter
1 tablespoon olive oil
1 teaspoon chopped shallot or white onion
1 small clove garlic, minced
⅓ cup white wine
⅓ cup Marsala wine
2 cups Brown Sauce
1 can (10½ ounces) condensed consommé
½ cup chopped ripe tomatoes
1 tablespoon minced parsley
1 bay leaf

Sauté mushrooms in butter and oil. Add shallot and
garlic and sauté for another 5 minutes or until pale
golden brown. Add white wine and Marsala. Cook at
a boil until half its original volume, about 15 minutes.
Add Brown Sauce, consommé, tomatoes, parsley, and
bay leaf. Simmer 15 minutes. Remove bay leaf. If
desired, sauce may be thickened with 2 tablespoons
cornstarch mixed with ¼ cup cold water. Makes about
4 cups of sauce.

Frogs' Legs Provençale à la Ernie's
Serves 4

4 pounds frogs' legs (24 legs) or 12 small
chicken drumsticks
Salt, pepper
1 can (10½ ounces) condensed cream of
celery soup
⅓ cup cream
Flour
½ cup butter
½ cup oil

46

⅓ cup white wine
1 small clove garlic, minced
½ cup butter
¼ cup chopped parsley
1 lemon, cut into thin slices

Wash frogs' legs or chicken drumsticks and pat dry. Sprinkle very lightly with salt and pepper. Press cream of celery soup through a sieve and mix with cream. Dip frogs' legs or drumsticks into soup mixture, coating them completely; drain excess. Roll legs in flour, coating completely. Heat butter and oil in a large skillet and brown legs on all sides. Sauté for 10 minutes for frogs' legs, 30 to 35 minutes for drumsticks. When tender, remove from skillet and place on a platter. Keep warm. Drain fat from skillet. Add white wine to skillet and bring to a boil, scraping pan. Add garlic, butter, and 1 tablespoon of the parsley; cook until butter turns golden brown. Spoon mixture over legs. Sprinkle with remaining parsley and top with lemon slices. Serve with boiled new potatoes.

Filet of Beef Elysian

Serves 8

1 filet of beef, about 3½ pounds, well trimmed
1 can (8 ounces) pâté de foie gras
1 can (⅞ ounce) truffles, sliced
Salt, pepper
Suet in thin sheets to wrap around filet
1 carrot, chopped
1 onion, chopped
½ teaspoon crumbled thyme
1 bay leaf
1 clove garlic, chopped
1 cup Marsala wine
1 cup Brown Sauce
8 pieces endive, braised
⅓ cup grated Parmesan cheese
1 cup button mushrooms, sautéed in butter

Cut filet crosswise into 8 slices, cutting not all the way through. Cut pâté into 8 slices and stuff one slice into each cut. Add truffle slices. Sprinkle filet with salt and pepper. Wrap meat with suet and tie with string. Roast in a shallow pan in a preheated 450°F. oven for 30 minutes. Add carrot, onion, thyme, bay leaf, and garlic. Roast another 5 minutes. Remove from pan and keep warm. Add Marsala and Brown Sauce to pan and bring to a boil, scraping to loosen all bits in pan. Simmer for 10 minutes. Remove suet from meat and place meat on a platter. Surround with endive sprinkled with Parmesan cheese and button mushrooms. Strain sauce and spoon sauce over meat and vegetables. Cut slices of filet between slashes stuffed with pâté. Garnish with watercress.

Cornish Game Hen à l'Orange

Serves 4

Salt, pepper
1 Cornish game hen, about 3 pounds
(or roasting chicken)
1 can (1 pound) onions, drained
2 tablespoons butter
½ teaspoon salt
Dash sugar
2 navel oranges
Boiling water
1 carrot, chopped
½ teaspoon thyme
1 bay leaf
Dash ground cloves
¼ cup port wine
¼ cup Brown Sauce
1 can (10½ ounces) condensed chicken broth
1½ tablespoons red currant jelly

Sprinkle salt and pepper inside and outside of game hen. Roast in a shallow pan in a preheated 400°F. oven for 30 minutes. Glaze onions in butter, adding salt and sugar. Peel orange thinly, using a sharp knife and removing as little of the white membrane as possible. Shred peel and cover with boiling water. Let stand. Add carrot, onion, thyme, bay leaf, and cloves to game hen and roast another 10 minutes. Add port wine and Brown Sauce and roast until bird is tender. Remove game hen to a platter and keep warm. Strain sauce in pan with fowl and pour into a saucepan. Add chicken broth and drained orange rind. Bring to a boil and stir in jelly. Spoon glazed onions around game hen. Slice orange after removing white membrane and place around game hen. If desired, garnish with sautéed mushroom caps and brandied cherries. Spoon sauce over game hen. Serve with wild rice.

Sauce Bercy

½ cup white wine
2 tablespoons chopped shallots or white onions
¼ teaspoon ground black pepper
1½ cups Brown Sauce
⅔ cup butter, at room temperature
3 tablespoons chopped parsley

Combine wine and shallots and boil until shallots are tender. Add pepper and cook until ¼ original liquid remains in pan. Stir in Brown Sauce. Cool. Mash butter and mix until soft and fluffy. Beat in wine sauce and chopped parsley. Serve on boiled meat or broiled or baked fish. Makes 2½ cups of sauce.

The *Greenbrier*

The warmth of old-style Southern hospitality lives on at the beautiful Greenbrier, a magnificent 6,500-acre resort in the West Virginia hills. The Greenbrier dining rooms offer the diner two pleasures: wonderful views of gently rolling mountains and food exquisitely prepared and served. The unparalleled choice of dishes, served in the grand manner, has made the resort a favorite dining place for the eighteen Presidents of the United States who have been guests at The Greenbrier. The executive food director, Herman G. Rusch, is a member of the Order of the Golden Dozen, composed of the world's greatest chefs, and many of the chefs who serve under him are award winners as well; understandably, The Greenbrier's cuisine is internationally famous.

Striped Bass Ma Façon

Serves 6

6 to 7 pound sea bass, filleted
Salt, pepper
½ cup melted butter
1 tablespoon minced onion
2 tablespoons lemon juice
2 cups Chablis wine
1 can (10 ounces) frozen condensed
oyster stew, thawed
1 can (10½ ounces) condensed cream of
asparagus soup

Cut each of the bass fillets into three pieces and sprinkle with salt and pepper. Place fish pieces in a shallow pan in a single layer. Add butter, onion, lemon juice, wine, and liquid drained from oyster stew. (Reserve oysters.) Bake in a preheated 400°F. oven 20 minutes or until fish flakes. Remove fish carefully and place on a platter and keep warm. Transfer liquid in baking dish to a saucepan and boil until liquid is reduced to one-third of its original volume. Add asparagus soup and continue simmering until sauce is thick. Add oysters and reheat slightly. Spoon sauce over fish. Garnish with parsley.

Sauce Robert

4 strips bacon, finely chopped
2 cans (10½ ounces each) condensed onion soup
½ cup wine vinegar
2 teaspoons sugar
2 tablespoons Dijon mustard
¼ cup butter
¼ cup flour

Fry bacon in a saucepan until crisp. Add onion soup, wine vinegar, sugar, and mustard. Stir until mixture comes to a boil. Mix butter and flour until a paste is formed. Drop the lump of butter and flour into the hot sauce. Cook over low heat, stirring, until sauce bubbles and thickens. Spoon over hot slices of beef, lamb, veal, or pork. Makes 3½ cups of sauce.

Left: Striped Bass Ma Façon

Adapted by Executive Food Director Herman G. Rusch.

Sweet-Sour Pork Tenderloin

Serves 6

¼ cup butter
12 slices pork tenderloin, well trimmed,
½-inch thick
Salt, pepper
Sweet-Sour Sauce

Melt butter in a large skillet. Season pork with salt and pepper. Brown meat on both sides and sauté slowly, about 15 to 20 minutes, until meat is almost cooked. Add Sweet-Sour Sauce and simmer for another 15 minutes. Serve slices of pork with pan juices spooned over them.

Sweet-Sour Sauce

1 cup sugar
½ cup white vinegar
Demi-Glacé Sauce
1 tablespoon cornstarch mixed with
2 tablespoons water

Add sugar to vinegar and stir to blend. Cook at a boil until liquid turns a golden brown. Slowly add Demi-Glacé Sauce. (Mixture will bubble violently.) Stir to blend. Stir in cornstarch mixture and cook, stirring, until sauce is thickened. Makes about 2½ cups of sauce.

50

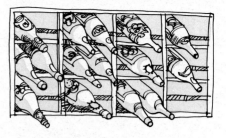

Demi-Glacé Sauce

1 can (10½ ounces) condensed beef broth
⅓ cup country-style tomato juice
1 clove garlic, minced
Pinch marjoram
Pinch rosemary
½ bay leaf
2 whole cloves
⅓ cup Madeira wine

Combine all ingredients and simmer for 15 minutes. Strain and store in the refrigerator for use as the base of most brown sauces. Makes about 1½ cups of sauce.

Veal Roast Suédoise

Serves 6

1 veal leg roast, about 3½ pounds
Salt, pepper
1 can (10¾ ounces) condensed vegetable and beef
stockpot soup
1 cup white wine
Supreme Sauce

Sprinkle meat with salt and pepper. Place meat into a Dutch oven and add stockpot soup and wine. Cover tightly and simmer for 2 hours or until meat is tender. Remove meat and keep warm. Simmer sauce until reduced to half its original volume. Stir in Supreme Sauce. Slice meat and pour some of the hot sauce over each serving.

Supreme Sauce

1 can (10½ ounces) condensed golden
mushroom soup
¼ cup white wine
¼ cup light cream
1 tablespoon lemon juice

Combine all ingredients, simmer, stirring constantly, until sauce is smooth and bubbly. Makes about 1½ cups of sauce.

GENE'S LOBSTER HOUSE

The chief commodity of Madeira Beach—a part of St. Petersburg, Florida—is sunshine. Until recently this was largely a retirement community, popular too as a tourist stop. But the recent growth of industry is bringing young families to the city. The Aquarium, with its performing sea lions and porpoises and hundreds of varieties of sea life, and Florida's Sunken Gardens, with their displays of lush tropical flowering plants and a large collection of gay-plumaged birds, are both worth a visit. And so is Gene's Lobster House, where seafood, prepared with exquisite care, is served in two informal, nautically decorated dining rooms. Both these rooms, and the bar as well, house a display of boating antiques and are furnished with captain's tables and chairs collected from all over the world. Maine lobster is a specialty, but the rarer Danish and African lobsters are also features of the menu, and there is a wide variety of seafood dishes of all kinds, including a particularly delicious Shrimp au Gratin.

Danish Lobster Tetrazzini

Serves 6

2 cans (10½ ounces each) condensed cream of
mushroom soup
⅔ cup (10¾-ounce can) condensed tomato soup
3 cups cooked, shelled, and diced lobster
½ pound thin spaghetti
½ cup grated Parmesan cheese
½ cup grated sharp Cheddar cheese
2 tablespoons dry bread crumbs

Combine and heat mushroom and tomato soups. Add lobster meat and cook for 5 minutes. Cook spaghetti in boiling water until firm but tender. Drain and rinse with boiling water. Pour spaghetti into a well-greased 2-quart casserole; spoon lobster mixture over spaghetti. Combine remaining ingredients and sprinkle over top of casserole. Bake in a preheated 375°F. oven for 15 minutes or until browned on top. This casserole may be prepared ahead of time and refrigerated—allow 25 to 30 minutes cooking time.

Shrimp au Gratin en Casserole

Serves 4 to 6

2 tablespoons butter
2 tablespoons flour
1 cup milk
½ teaspoon salt
⅛ teaspoon pepper
1 can (10¾ ounces) condensed Cheddar cheese soup
1 pound shrimp, cooked, shelled, and deveined
1 cup grated Swiss or Cheddar cheese

Melt butter and stir in flour. Gradually stir in milk. Add salt and pepper. Cook, stirring, until sauce bubbles and thickens. Add soup and shrimp. Stir again until sauce bubbles. Pour mixture into a greased 1-quart casserole. Sprinkle top with cheese. Bake casserole in a preheated 400°F. oven for 10 minutes or until cheese is melted and the Shrimp au Gratin is thoroughly heated.

Adapted by Chef George Bawkin.

Jackson Lake Lodge

Jackson Lake, in Grand Teton National Park, Wyoming, acts as a reflecting pool for the awesome, snowcapped mountains that surround it. The park itself is a wild solitude, breathtaking in the grandeur of its peaks and the clear blue of its lakes. Many river and lake trips are offered visitors, as well as guided hikes and walks along carefully marked nature trails, and daytime and moonlight cruises on Jackson Lake feature campfire cookouts. Situated at the foot of Grand Teton Mountain is Jackson Lake Lodge, a gift to the United States from John D. Rockefeller, Jr.—as was the park itself. A favorite vacation spot for families, the Lodge prepares meals for hearty appetites, but manages with flair and expertise to keep them in the gourmet category.

Fresh Stuffed Artichokes

Serves 4

4 large fresh whole artichokes
1 cup chopped fresh mushrooms
¼ cup chopped shallots or white onions
1 tablespoon chopped chervil
1 tablespoon chopped chives
1 can (10½ ounces) condensed cream of
mushroom soup
1 tablespoon liquid meat extract
¼ cup grated Parmesan cheese
Paprika

Trim the spiny points from the artichoke leaves, using a pair of shears. Parboil. Combine mushrooms, shallots, chervil, chives, mushroom soup, and liquid meat extract. Stuff the mushroom mixture between the leaves and over the tops of the artichokes. Place artichokes in a shallow baking pan. Sprinkle with grated Parmesan cheese and paprika. Bake in a preheated 350°F. oven for 40 to 45 minutes, or until an artichoke is easily pierced through to the bottom.

Left: Fresh Stuffed Artichokes

Calves' Brains Beaumont, Argentenile

Serves 4

2 calves' brains, separated into halves
Water
1 tablespoon salt
1 can (2¾ ounces) purée de foie gras truffe
1 cup white wine
2 shallots or 1 small white onion, chopped
1 can (10½ ounces) condensed cream of
asparagus soup
Chopped chervil

Cover brains with water; add salt; simmer until brains are white and firm. Drain and cover with cold water. Remove excess membranes and slice each brain half into halves lengthwise. Spread 4 slices of brains with pâté and top with second 4 slices. Combine wine and shallots in a skillet and simmer for 5 minutes. Stir in asparagus soup. Gently place brains into sauce and spoon sauce over. Cook gently until hot. Serve sprinkled with a little chopped chervil.

Adapted by Chef Franz Nikodemus.

La Fonda

The beauties of Santa Fe, oldest capital city in the country, are surpassed only by those of the Sangre de Cristo Mountains, towering high above the town. Founded by Don Pedro de Peralta, who designed the Plaza and built the handsome Palace of Governors in 1609, Santa Fe by 1617 had become an important center, situated as it was at the confluence of four major western trails. The Plaza—the end of the Santa Fe Trail—was, and still is, the focus of the civic and social life of the city, which retains a strong Spanish influence in architecture, dress, and the arts. Here in the historic Plaza is La Fonda, dating from pioneer days and still maintaining many of the customs and traditions enjoyed by its earliest visitors. Decorated with rare pieces of art from Spain and Mexico, the restaurant offers a superb cuisine: a blend of Indian, Spanish, Anglo-American, and Mexican dishes meticulously prepared, graciously served.

Caprican Round Steak

Serves 6

1½ pounds round steak, cut ¼ inch thick
Salt, pepper
¼ cup butter
1 clove garlic, minced
2 cups fresh bread crumbs
3 tablespoons chopped parsley
2 hard-cooked eggs, chopped
¼ cup grated Parmesan cheese
¼ cup butter
1 can (10½ ounces) condensed onion soup
½ cup chopped fresh mushrooms
1 cup Burgundy wine

Pound steak until very thin, then cut into 6 long pieces large enough to roll around stuffing. Sprinkle meat with salt and pepper. Heat ¼ cup butter and sauté garlic until golden. Add crumbs and sauté briefly until just golden brown. Stir in parsley, hard-cooked eggs, and Parmesan cheese. Spoon some of this mixture on each piece of round steak. Roll up and fasten with a toothpick. Brown meat on all sides in a large skillet in ¼ cup butter. Add onion soup, mushrooms, and wine. Cover and simmer until meat is tender, about 1 hour. Thicken pan drippings if desired with flour mixed with water. Serve with noodles.

Harvey's Tomatonion Soup

Serves 6

1 can (10½ ounces) condensed onion soup
1 can (11 ounces) condensed bisque of tomato soup
1 can (10½ ounces) condensed chicken broth
2 soup cans water
1 bay leaf
2 tablespoons chopped parsley
1 tablespoon chopped chives

Combine all ingredients in a saucepan and simmer for 15 minutes. Remove bay leaf. Serve hot, sprinkled with additional chopped chives.

Adaptations of traditional recipes.

Chili Con Carne

Serves 4 to 6

2 tablespoons vegetable shortening
2 pounds coarsely ground lean chuck
2 cloves garlic, mashed
1½ teaspoons crumbled oregano
2 tablespoons flour
2 cans (11 ounces each) condensed
chili beef soup
1 can (10½ ounces) condensed beef broth
½ cup diced pimiento
Salt

Heat shortening in a deep saucepan. Add beef and cook until meat is crumbly and well browned. Add garlic, oregano, and flour. Stir to blend. Add chili beef soup, beef broth, and pimiento. Stir to blend and heat until bubbly. Season to taste with salt.

Breast of Chicken Lucrecio

Serves 8

8 chicken breast halves
Salt, pepper
¼ cup butter

Sauce

3 tablespoons butter
1 pound chuck, cut into ½-inch cubes
¼ cup minced onion
1 clove garlic, minced
¼ cup flour
½ teaspoon cumin seeds
1 cup finely chopped red Mexican chilies
1 can (10½ ounces) condensed chicken broth
1 can (10½ ounces) condensed beef broth
1½ cups water
2 cans (6 ounces each) country-style tomato juice
1 teaspoon oregano
½ cup toasted slivered almonds

Sprinkle chicken breasts with salt and pepper. Sauté chicken in a skillet in hot ¼ cup butter. When brown, cover and simmer over low heat until tender, about 35 minutes. Meanwhile in a saucepan melt 3 tablespoons butter. Brown chuck. Add onion and garlic during last minutes as meat browns. Sprinkle flour over meat. Add remaining ingredients except almonds and simmer, covered, for 1 hour or until meat is tender. Strain sauce; set chuck aside for other uses. Pour sauce over chicken breasts. Cover and simmer for 30 minutes. Sprinkle with toasted slivered almonds.

Veal Cutlet, Española

Serves 8

8 large veal scaloppini, about 1½ pounds, Italian
style or pounded thin
Salt, pepper
Flour
2 eggs, well beaten
2 cups dry bread crumbs
½ cup butter
1 can (10¾ ounces) condensed
tomato soup, heated
2 ripe avocados, peeled and sliced
8 ounces Mozzarella cheese

Sprinkle veal on both sides with salt and pepper. Dip slices into flour, then into beaten eggs, and then into crumbs. Press crumbs firmly against meat. Melt butter in a large skillet and brown meat on both sides. Place slices of veal side by side in a shallow broiler pan. Spoon hot soup on·top of veal. Top with slices of avocado. Cover avocado with slices of cheese. Place under broiler and broil until cheese is melted and lightly browned.

Santa Fe Omelette

Serves 4

6 eggs
½ teaspoon salt
¼ teaspoon pepper
2 canned green chilies, diced and peeled
¼ cup butter
1 can (10¾ ounces) condensed Cheddar cheese soup
½ cup light cream

Beat eggs with salt and pepper until well blended and slightly foamy. Fold in chilies. Melt butter in a 10-inch skillet. Pour in egg mixture. Cook until set, lifting edge of omelette to allow uncooked portion to run underneath. While omelette is cooking heat cheese soup with cream until bubbly. Fold omelette onto a platter. Spoon hot sauce over omelette.

India house

As communications and transportation draw the four corners of the world closer together, experiences that were once exceptional become commonplace. Japanese gardens proliferate in the Middle West; carvings from the Congo are sold in Wyoming. And exotic foods that at one time could be sampled only by far-ranging travelers can now be enjoyed thousands of miles from their origins. There is almost no sizable city in the United States that does not offer an Indian restaurant. Yet somehow the seaport cities still have an edge on the atmosphere that goes along with such food—the cities which, at one time, spun the only threads of contact between East and West. Such a city is San Francisco, which has one of the finest Indian restaurants in this country, India House. Owned by David Brown and his wife, India House preserves an old tradition with its authentic atmosphere. There is a very "Pukka Sahib" English Colonial bar. Indian students in their native dress serve the many delightful dishes on the thoroughly Indian menu, which features—naturally—many tasty curries as well as a variety of other specialties to stretch the gustatory horizons of American diners.

Indian Curry

Serves 2 to 3

¼ cup chopped onion
1 clove garlic, minced
2 to 4 teaspoons curry powder
2 tablespoons butter or margarine
1 can (10 ounces) frozen condensed cream of
shrimp soup
1 cup light cream
1 cup cooked crab meat

Cook onion, garlic, and curry powder in butter until onion is tender. Add soup and cream. Heat until soup is thawed, stirring often. Add crab meat. Serve with hot fluffy rice and bowls of chutney, grated coconut, chopped cucumber, slivered almonds, and quartered limes. (Diced chicken, shrimp, or quartered hard-cooked eggs can be substituted for the crab meat.)

Left: Indian Curry

Senegalese Soup

Serves 4 to 6

¼ cup chopped onion
1 medium clove garlic, minced
2 teaspoons curry powder
1 tablespoon butter or margarine
1 can (11¼ ounces) condensed green pea soup
1 can (10½ ounces) condensed cream of
chicken soup
1½ soup cans milk
Cucumber or apple slices

In a saucepan, cook onion with garlic and curry in butter until tender. Gradually blend in soups and milk until smooth. Cook 5 minutes; stir now and then. Chill. Stir before serving. Thin with additional milk, if desired. Garnish with cucumber or apple slices.

Adapted by Owners David and Patricia Brown.

The Golden Lion

Seattle is a seaport town, a gateway to the Orient, a city that retains a feeling of historical adventure even though it is very much a part of the space age. It seems a fit setting for the lush splendor of The Golden Lion, a restaurant designed to recreate the glory of British colonialism at its height, when far-ranging British ships were opening to Western civilization the mysteries of the East. Against the red tapestry walls of the multi-level room, waiters in East Indian dress stand out brilliantly, enhancing the appeal of international gourmet dishes and the flaming-sword specialties of the house—the exotic spectaculars of which The Golden Lion is justly proud.

Crab Legs St. Denis
Serves 4

*2 packages (12 ounces each) crab legs,
fresh, or frozen, thawed
2 tablespoons butter
1 shallot, minced, or 2 tablespoons minced
white onion
1 can (10½ ounces) condensed cream of
mushroom soup
¼ cup white wine
¼ cup heavy cream
1 teaspoon chopped chives or parsley
1 cup flour
1 egg, well beaten
1 cup fine dry bread crumbs
½ cup butter*

Remove crab meat from shells in one piece. Drain well. Melt 2 tablespoons butter and sauté shallot until tender (not brown). Stir in soup, wine, cream, and chives. Simmer until bubbly. Pat crab legs dry and dip into flour, then beaten egg, then into crumbs, pressing crumbs so they adhere. Melt ½ cup butter and sauté crab until richly browned and crisp. Spoon sauce into a shallow casserole. Place crab legs on top, covering sauce. Garnish with parsley sprigs.

Golden Lion Soup
Serves 6

*cans (10 ounces each) frozen condensed oyster stew
2 teaspoons curry powder
1 cup heavy cream
4 egg yolks
50 shucked Olympia oysters (these are the very
tiny oysters) or 2 cups quartered oysters
1 cup heavy cream, whipped*

Heat stew just to thaw and combine with curry powder. Mix cream and egg yolks, and stir mixture into oyster stew. Cook over low heat, stirring constantly, until stew thickens slightly; do not boil. Stir in oysters and simmer for 5 minutes or until edges of oysters curl. Spoon stew into bowls. Top with whipped cream. Place under broiler and broil 1 to 2 minutes. Serve the soup at once.

Left: Crab Legs St. Denis

Adaptations from recipes by Chef René Schiess.

Jockey Club

In the Fairfax Hotel in Washington, D.C., is the handsome Jockey Club. Although it derives its name from one of the world's most famous establishments, in Madrid, and some of its décor from New York's equally famous "21," it has a personality and a menu all its own. It could hardly be otherwise in a restaurant that serves so special a group of diners: the top-ranking newsmakers of the first city of the nation, gathering there to be catered to by one of its top chefs.

Wild Boar

Serves 6

1 can (10½ ounces) condensed consommé
2 cups cider vinegar
8 cups red wine
1½ teaspoons ground black pepper
2 tablespoons salt
2 bay leaves
1 teaspoon crumbled thyme
2 cloves garlic, chopped
8 juniper berries
1 piece wild boar meat, about 5 pounds
6 carrots, scraped and quartered
2 large onions, quartered
4 stalks celery, cut into 2-inch lengths
1 can (10½ ounces) condensed beef broth
⅓ cup currant jelly
½ cup flour mixed with ¾ cup water

Combine consommé, vinegar, wine, pepper, salt, bay leaves, thyme, garlic, and juniper berries in a glass or enamel bowl. Place boar meat into marinade. Let marinate for 2 days at room temperature. Place meat and marinade in a large kettle. Cover and simmer for 2 to 2½ hours or until meat is almost tender. Add carrots, onions, celery. Cover and simmer until vegetables are tender, about 20 minutes. Remove meat and vegetables and keep warm. Add beef broth, currant jelly, and flour mixture to pan liquid. Stir until sauce bubbles and thickens slightly. Let sauce cook at a boil until it becomes the thickness of a good brown gravy. Pour hot gravy over portions of sliced boar and vegetables. Serve with Chestnut Purée.

Chestnut Purée

Serves 6

2 cans (11 ounces each) whole chestnuts, drained
½ cup finely chopped celery
1 can (10½ ounces) condensed consommé
1 tablespoon butter
⅓ cup light cream

In a saucepan combine chestnuts, celery, and consommé. Boil until consommé is absorbed. Press chestnuts through a sieve or whirl in a blender. Stir in butter and cream. Serve with Wild Boar. *Note:* Chestnut Purée is also an excellent accompaniment for turkey, filet of beef, and lamb.

Left: Wild Boar, Chestnut Purée, Stuffed Tomatoes, Lobster Crêpes

Adaptations from recipes by Chef Claude Bouchet.

Andrew Jackson named Memphis, on the Mississippi, after the Egyptian Memphis on the Nile. A synthesis of the slow charm of the Old South and the bustle of a modern metropolis, Memphis today offers such contrasts as Old Beale Street, where W. C. Handy gave birth to the blues, and a handsome modern civic center. A stately French Colonial mansion in Old Coward Place houses Justines, where the beautifully served food is as delightful as the setting. Walls of handmade brick set in herringbone pattern, old wrought-iron window guards, settees and balustrades fill Justines with the grace of another day. Stately candelabra, damask, pier glasses, and paintings by fine artists add to the charm. The menu offers a wide selection of traditional dishes of the region. There is also a Justines in Atlanta, Georgia.

Stuffed Fish Mornay

Serves 4

1 can (10¾ ounces) condensed
Cheddar cheese soup
½ cup flaked crab meat
½ cup chopped shrimp
2 tablespoons chopped mushrooms
2 tablespoons chopped green onions
¼ teaspoon salt
¼ teaspoon tarragon, crushed
½ small clove garlic, minced
8 fillets of flounder, about 2 pounds (or fillet of
sole, red snapper, ocean perch, or pompano)
8 oysters, cut in half
2 tablespoons melted butter
¼ cup water
2 tablespoons diced tomato
Generous dash crushed tarragon

In bowl, combine ¼ cup soup with crab, shrimp, mushrooms, onions, salt, tarragon, and garlic. Mix well. Arrange four fillets in shallow baking dish; spread evenly with filling. Top with oysters. Cover with remaining fillets. Brush with melted butter. Bake in preheated 375°F. oven for 30 minutes. For sauce, combine remaining soup with water, tomato, and tarragon. Heat, stirring now and then. Serve with fish. Makes 1 cup sauce. *Onion Sauce:* Omit tomato; substitute 1 tablespoon finely chopped green onion.

Watercress Soup

Serves 6

½ cup butter
½ cup finely chopped leeks
1 can (10½ ounces) condensed cream of
potato soup
1 can (10½ ounces) condensed chicken broth
1 cup milk
1 cup light cream
1 tablespoon chopped parsley
1 bunch watercress, stems removed
and chopped finely

Heat butter and sauté leeks until tender but not brown. Add soups, milk, cream, parsley, and watercress. Simmer for 5 minutes. Serve hot.

Left: Beef Wellington, Stuffed Fish Mornay,
Lobster Thermidor

Adapted by Owner Dayton Smith.

Spinach Ring

Serves 6

2 sets calves' brains
3 pounds fresh spinach, cooked and chopped fine
2 hard-cooked eggs, sieved
1 egg, well beaten
6 tablespoons melted butter
Juice of ½ lemon
1 tablespoon flour
¼ cup heavy cream
1 teaspoon baking powder
1 teaspoon salt
¼ teaspoon pepper
1 can (10½ ounces) condensed cream of
mushroom soup
1 teaspoon grated onion
¾ cup grated sharp Cheddar cheese
¼ cup heavy cream

Cover brains with cold water. Bring water to a boil and cook until brains are firm, about 20 minutes. Drain and drench with cold water. Carefully remove membranes. Press brains through a sieve or whirl in a blender. Stir in spinach, hard-cooked eggs, beaten egg, melted butter, lemon juice, flour, heavy cream, baking powder, salt, and pepper. Pour mixture into a well-buttered 6-cup ring mold. Bake in a preheated 350°F. oven for 1 hour or until firm. Turn out of mold. For sauce, combine remaining ingredients and simmer until sauce is smooth and cheese is melted. Serve with sauce on ring.

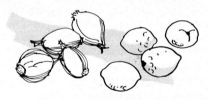

Asparagus Soup

Serves 4

2 cans (10½ ounces each) condensed cream of
asparagus soup
2 cups light cream
1 package (10 ounces) frozen asparagus spears,
thawed, or 2 cups fresh asparagus tips, cooked
Salt, pepper, sugar

Combine all ingredients in a blender and whirl until smooth. Pour into a saucepan and heat just until bubbly. Season to taste with salt, pepper, and a few grains of sugar.

Tomato-Celery Soup

Serves 2 to 3

1 cup finely chopped celery
2 tablespoons butter or margarine
1 can (10¾ ounces) condensed tomato soup
1 cup milk

In saucepan, cook celery in butter until tender. Stir in soup and milk. Heat, stirring now and then. Serve with croutons if desired.

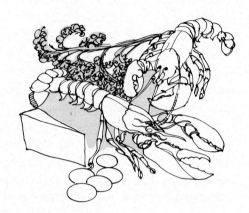

Lobster Thermidor

Serves 4

4 lobsters, about 1½ pounds each
½ cup butter
1 teaspoon paprika
2 tablespoons flour
½ cup sherry
1 can (10½ ounces) condensed cream of
mushroom soup
2 egg yolks
1½ cups grated Cheddar cheese

Drop lobsters into boiling salted water. Cook until lobster shells turn red, about 10 minutes. Drain and drench with cold water. Split lobsters lengthwise and remove tomalley and lobster meat found in the claws, body, and tail. Dice meat. Melt butter in a skillet and add diced lobster and tomalley. Sprinkle with paprika and flour. Stir to blend. Stir in sherry. Mix mushroom soup and egg yolks, and stir into lobster mixture. Cook over low heat, stirring constantly, until sauce bubbles and thickens. Place lobster shells on a heatproof platter. Spoon lobster and sauce into shells. Sprinkle with grated cheese. Place under broiler; broil until cheese melts and becomes golden brown.

64

Glasgow Arms

With its population of a hundred persons, Glasgow is an unspoiled, pretty little town. It was the site of the only battle of the Revolution fought on Delaware soil, and here, on September 3, 1777, Betsy Ross's first flag was raised. Present-day pride of the town is the Glasgow Arms, founded in 1937 and still operated by its original owner. The restaurant's name and crest are taken from the Coat of Arms of Glasgow, Scotland, by permission of the Lord Provost. Decorating the restaurant are paintings done by members of the owner's family and interesting displays of old arms and other handsome craft pieces, some of them dating from as early as the fifteenth century.

Tenderloin of Beef Stroganoff with Wild Rice

Serves 6

6 slices beef tenderloin, about 1 inch thick
⅓ cup butter
1 carrot, finely chopped
½ cup finely chopped celery
1 tablespoon finely chopped onion
½ teaspoon dill seeds
3 tablespoons flour
1 can (10½ ounces) condensed beef broth or consommé
1 tablespoon tomato catsup
¼ cup Sauternes
½ cup sour cream
4½ cups cooked wild rice

Sauté beef slices in butter until medium rare. Place on a platter and keep warm. To drippings in pan, add carrot, celery, onion, and dill. When vegetables are tender, stir in flour. Gradually stir in beef broth, tomato catsup, and wine. Cook over low heat, stirring constantly, until sauce bubbles and thickens. Press sauce through a sieve or whirl in a blender. Reheat and stir in sour cream. Heat but do not boil. Spoon sauce over meat slices, which have been placed over hot wild rice.

Alaskan King Crab Meat Newburg en Casserole

Serves 4

2 packages (6 ounces each) frozen king crab meat
2 tablespoons butter
½ bay leaf, crumbled
Pinch crumbled thyme
½ teaspoon paprika
1 can (10½ ounces) cream of chicken soup
¼ cup sherry
Pepper
Toast points or cooked rice

Defrost king crab and drain well. Sauté crab meat in butter with bay leaf, thyme, and paprika until hot, about 5 minutes. Stir in soup and sherry. Season to taste with pepper. Simmer 5 minutes. Remove bay leaf. Simmer 5 minutes. Spoon over toast points or hot cooked rice.

Adaptations from recipes by Vice President John Sclavos.

Karl Ratzsch's

For thirty-nine years any gastronome who knows Milwaukee has found his way, as often as possible, to Karl Ratzsch's Old World Restaurant. Here the German-Continental food is of such magnificence that visitors from the old country itself have been moved to confess that the fabled restaurants back home provide no better. Karl Ratzsch's consistently ranks high on surveys of top restaurants; a well-known travel guidebook describes it as so outstanding that it is "worth a special effort to reach."

Pork Tenderloin Cordon Bleu à la Maria Christine

Serves 6

12 pork tenderloin slices, ½ inch thick or
thin-sliced center-cut pork
chops, bone removed
6 slices Emmenthaler cheese
6 slices smoked ham
Flour
1 egg, well beaten
2 tablespoons water
1½ cups cracker crumbs
Oil or shortening, 1 inch deep
2 cans (10½ ounces each) condensed golden
mushroom soup
⅔ cup heavy cream

Pound meat slices until very thin. Top 6 of the slices with a slice of cheese and a slice of ham cut slightly smaller in size than the tenderloin. Top with remaining meat slices. Press together. Dip meat carefully into flour on both sides, then dip into egg beaten with water. Dip into crumbs, pressing firmly to make crumbs adhere. Fry slowly in oil or shortening, about 45 minutes, so pork has time to be thoroughly cooked and is richly browned. Drain on absorbent paper. In a saucepan combine soup and cream; heat until bubbly. Serve tenderloin topped with sauce.

Left: Pork Tenderloin Cordon Bleu à la
Maria Christine

Braised Lamb Shanks Gemüse

Serves 6

6 lamb shanks, about ¾ to 1 pound each
⅓ cup butter
2 bay leaves
2 mashed cloves garlic
12 peppercorns
¼ teaspoon each summer savory, thyme, marjoram
1 cup diced onion
1 cup diced celery
1 cup diced carrots
1 can (10¾ ounces) condensed vegetable and
beef stockpot soup
1 cup red wine
1 cup water
1 package (10 ounces) frozen peas
1 package (9 ounces) frozen cut green beans

Brown lamb shanks in butter. Add remaining ingredients except peas and green beans. Stir to blend. Cover and simmer slowly until lamb shanks are tender, adding water from time to time as necessary to prevent sticking. Add peas and green beans and simmer covered until vegetables are tender, about 10 minutes. Remove bay leaves. If desired thicken gravy with 1 tablespoon flour mixed with ¼ cup water.

Adapted by Chef Raymond Drews.

Purée of Mongole Soup

Serves 8 to 10

1 pound (2 cups) yellow split peas
1 medium onion, diced
2 large carrots, diced
1 cup sliced celery
1 teaspoon white pepper
1 tablespoon salt
¼ teaspoon grated nutmeg
1 can (10½ ounces) condensed consommé
1 can (10¾ ounces) condensed tomato soup
10 cups water
1 smoked ham hock

Combine all ingredients in a large kettle. Bring to a boil, lower heat and simmer for 1 hour or until split peas are very soft. Remove ham hock. Press soup through a sieve or food mill or whirl in a blender. Serve garnished with finely chopped parsley and crisp croutons.

68

Lichtenstein Casserole

Serves 6

4 pounds tenderloin tips or boneless beef chuck, cut into 1-inch cubes
½ cup butter
2 medium onions, cut into slices
1 pound button mushrooms, stems removed
½ cup flour
1 cup dry red wine
2 cans (10½ ounces each) condensed onion soup
2 soup cans water
Salt, pepper

In a Dutch oven sauté beef cubes in butter until brown on all sides. Add onions and mushrooms; sauté until vegetables are wilted. Sprinkle with flour. Stir in red wine, onion soup, and water. Stir to blend. Cover and put into a preheated 325°F. oven 45 to 50 minutes for tenderloin and 1½ to 2 hours for beef chuck. Remove from oven and season to taste with salt and pepper. Garnish with chopped parsley; surround with peas and tiny whole baby carrots.

Veal Kidney Stew

Serves 6

6 veal kidneys
Salt, pepper
¼ cup butter
1 cup diced carrots
1 cup diced onions
1 cup sliced celery
¼ cup flour
¾ cup Burgundy wine
1 can (10¾ ounces) condensed old-fashioned vegetable soup
1 can (10½ ounces) condensed beef broth

Soak kidneys in cold water for 30 minutes. Slice, removing all gristle and tubes. Season and brown slices quickly in butter in a large skillet over high heat. Remove cooked kidneys to a platter and reserve. Add carrots, onions, and celery to pan drippings and sauté until vegetables are wilted. Sprinkle with flour. Stir in wine, vegetable soup, and beef broth. Cook over low heat, stirring occasionally, until vegetables are tender. Add kidneys and simmer until sauce bubbles. Serve with rice or noodles.

Horseradish Sauce

1 can (10½ ounces) condensed cream of celery soup
2 to 4 tablespoons white horseradish, according to taste
2 to 4 tablespoons white vinegar, according to taste
2 tablespoons sugar
¼ cup dry white wine
Salt, white pepper

Combine all ingredients in a saucepan, seasoning to taste with salt and pepper. Heat until bubbly. Serve on boiled or roast beef, boiled brisket, tongue, corned beef, and roast fresh pork. Makes about 2 cups of horseradish sauce.

hoyt's
The DINNER BELL

In 1706 the governor of New Mexico moved thirty families from Bernalillo to a place where, he was told, there was better pasturage—a lovely, mountain-surrounded spot on the Rio Grande. Near the end of the eighteenth century this place, named Albuquerque, had a population of nearly six thousand. It had become a very large city for New Mexico at that time, and it is today still the largest city in the state. Nearby is Cibola National Forest, with its more than a million and a half scenic acres. Worth seeing are the Old Town, with its Spanish plaza, and the nearby Santa Ana, San Ildefonso, and Isleta pueblos, all open to the public during daylight hours. An excellent place to dine after a day's sight-seeing is The Dinner Bell—a name chosen by Claudine and Gwynn Hoyt, when they opened their restaurant more than twenty years ago, because it was reminiscent of early western tradition. In those bygone days the local restaurateur rang his dinner bell as the railroad train, then dinerless, pulled into the station. The Dinner Bell now has expanded to accommodate 250 guests in three dining rooms, each with its unique atmosphere. The menu is Continental-American; savory specialties of both cuisines reflect the blending of old world and new.

Chicken Livers Naomi

Serves 6

1 pound chicken livers
Flour
¼ cup butter
8 large mushroom caps, sliced
1 can (10½ ounces) condensed cream of chicken soup
½ cup Burgundy wine
Pinch thyme
Salt, pepper
6 patty shells or *toast slices*

Dredge chicken livers with flour. Melt butter in large skillet. Sauté the chicken livers until brown and barely cooked. Add mushrooms. Cover and cook gently for about five minutes. Stir in soup, Burgundy, and thyme. Season to taste with salt and pepper. Cook, stirring, just until mixture bubbles. Serve hot in patty shells or over hot buttered toast.

Tomato Bisque à la Claudine

Serves 6

2 cans (11 ounces each) condensed bisque of tomato soup
1 cup heavy cream
1 cup sherry
½ teaspoon oregano
Salt, pepper, garlic powder

Combine all ingredients with salt, pepper, and garlic powder to taste. Simmer, stirring occasionally, until very hot, about 15 minutes. Serve topped with sour cream and croutons.

Adapted by Owner Gwynn Hoyt.

KON·TIKI

The diner at Kon-Tiki trades the everyday world of Cleveland for the exotic fare and island décor of Polynesia. A pool, a waterfall, a profusion of plants set the scene; the walls are decorated with tapa cloths, carvings, ancient weapons, shields, Tiki gods. And the food and drink, including many exotic and unique specialties of the house, offer unfamiliar delights to the armchair—or the dinner-table—traveler.

Pork Canton

Serves 4

2 tablespoons peanut oil
1 pound boneless, very lean, tender pork
1 green pepper, seeded and cut into 1-inch triangles
1 cup well-drained pineapple chunks
1 cup diagonally sliced celery
2 tablespoons tomato catsup
1 can (10½ ounces) condensed chicken broth
½ cup white vinegar
⅓ cup sugar
2 tablespoons cornstarch

In a large skillet heat oil just until it starts to smoke. Add pork cut into ⅛-inch-thick strips. Stir quickly over high heat until pork is cooked, about 3 minutes. Add remaining ingredients except cornstarch. Cover and cook until vegetables are tender but crisp, about 6 minutes. Mix cornstarch and ¼ cup water; stir in quickly. Cook, stirring, until mixture bubbles and thickens. Season to taste with salt. Serve with hot rice.

Pea Pods and Water Chestnuts

Serves 6

2 tablespoons peanut oil
½ pound lean pork, cut into ⅛-inch strips

1 can (8 ounces) water chestnuts, drained and sliced
1 can (4 ounces) sliced mushrooms, drained
¼ cup thinly sliced bamboo shoots
¼ cup thinly sliced celery
1 can (10½ ounces) condensed chicken broth
1 pound Chinese pea pods, stringed and washed
or 2 packages (7 ounces each) frozen Chinese pea pods
2 tablespoons cornstarch
¼ cup water

In a large skillet heat oil just until it starts to smoke. Add pork and stir quickly over high heat until meat is cooked, about 3 minutes. Add water chestnuts, mushrooms, bamboo shoots, celery, and chicken broth. Stir to blend, lower heat and cover. Cook until celery is tender but still crisp. Add Chinese pea pods; cover and cook an additional 5 minutes. Pea pods must remain crisp. Mix cornstarch and water; stir quickly into mixture in skillet. Cook, stirring, until mixture bubbles and thickens. Season to taste with salt. Serve with hot rice. *For a spicier version* add 1 crushed clove garlic, 2 tablespoons soy sauce, and a dash of cayenne to the vegetables while they are cooking.

Left: Pork Canton

Adapted by Chef Bing Chen Chan.

Kungsholm

Stretching for twenty-five miles along Lake Michigan, Chicago is a major trade and transportation center and boasts the world's largest inland port. On one side lies the lake, fringed with green parks. The Loop, encircled by elevated train lines, is a city within a city; to the south are the docks and port. The North Side is the fashionable place to live—and to dine. The Kungsholm, Chicago's famous Scandinavian restaurant, operated by Fred Harvey, Inc., is noted both for its fine food and for its charming miniature theater. Decorated in red and gold, the unique theater offers opera favorites and popular musicals to an audience that can number only a few over two hundred. In the restaurant are individual areas for the enjoyment of the Kungsholm's outstanding smorgasbord, and for its varied, delicious Continental food.

73

Danish Roast Leg of Lamb

Serves 6 to 8

1 leg of lamb, 6 to 8 pounds
½ pound salt pork
Parsley
1 large head cauliflower
16 asparagus spears
1 pound small new potatoes, peeled
¼ cup butter
2 tablespoons sugar
1 can (10½ ounces) condensed cream of
celery soup
2 tablespoons lemon juice
2 tablespoons butter

Make about 6 slits in lamb. Stuff slits with small pieces of salt pork and parsley sprigs. Roast on a rack in a shallow pan in a preheated 325°F. oven for 3 to 4 hours for well-done lamb. Cook cauliflower, asparagus, and potatoes separately until tender. Heat butter and sugar in a skillet until mixture bubbles. Add well-drained new potatoes and keep turning over low heat until potatoes are richly browned. For sauce, whirl soup and lemon juice in a blender or press through a sieve. Add butter and simmer until hot. When meat is cooked, place on a large platter. Surround with vegetables. Spoon the hot sauce over the cauliflower and asparagus.

Cauliflower Salad

Serves 6

1 large cauliflower, core removed and thinly sliced
4 stalks celery, diced
1 can (10 ounces) frozen condensed cream of
shrimp soup, thawed
½ cup mayonnaise
Mandarin oranges

Combine cauliflower and celery in a salad bowl. Combine soup and mayonnaise and whirl in a blender until smooth. Pour dressing over salad and toss lightly. Chill until ready to serve. Garnish with mandarin orange sections.

Left: Danish Roast Leg of Lamb,
Cauliflower Salad

Adaptations of traditional recipes.

The Lemon Tree

In the heart of the Pennsylvania-Dutch country, the city of Lancaster is an astonishing blend of the old and the new. Once called the "arsenal of the Colonies," the town was a strategic stronghold during the Revolution. Today, amid the bustle of modern industrial Lancaster, the visitor will find much of Pennsylvania-Dutch life unchanged from the times of the early settlers. Just outside the city, in the verdant farmland, stands a lovely yellow-painted Pennsylvania-Dutch farmhouse, dating from 1858 and lovingly and meticulously restored by its present owners. This is The Lemon Tree, a restaurant of beauty and character. The diner who wants conventional food—steaks and chops—will not find it at The Lemon Tree, but he will find a varied and inventive international menu with dishes for the gastronomically adventurous, including The Lemon Tree's unique and mouth-watering Potato Almond Soup and other unusual dishes. No traveler forgets The Lemon Tree's food—or its charm.

Potato Almond Soup
Serves 4 to 5

1 can (10½ ounces) condensed cream of potato soup
1½ soup cans half-and-half
½ cup toasted slivered almonds
1 can (10½ ounces) condensed chicken broth
Dash pepper

Combine cream of potato soup, cream, and almonds in a blender container. Blend until smooth. Pour into a saucepan; add chicken broth and pepper. Heat, stirring now and then. Serve hot, garnished with snipped chives, watercress, or parsley.

Sweetbreads Amandine
Serves 6

2 pairs sweetbreads
2 bay leaves
1 teaspoon celery seed
2 tablespoons lemon juice
1 tablespoon olive oil
1 teaspoon curry powder
1 tablespoon finely chopped parsley
¼ cup slivered toasted almonds
¼ cup sliced stuffed olives
2 tablespoons port wine
2 cans (10½ ounces each) condensed cream of mushroom soup
6 patty shells

In a saucepan combine sweetbreads, bay leaves, celery seed, lemon juice, and enough water to cover. Bring to a boil; lower heat and simmer 5 minutes. Drain. Remove membranes and tubes and cut sweetbreads into bite-size pieces. In a skillet heat olive oil. Brown sweetbread pieces lightly. Add remaining ingredients except patty shells. Simmer until bubbly. Spoon sweetbread mixture over patty shells. Sprinkle with chopped parsley. Serve at once.

Left: Potato Almond Soup

Adaptations from recipes by Chef T. R. Chiffriller, Jr.

LONGFELLOW'S
Wayside Inn

The afterglow of history haunts Longfellow's Wayside Inn in South Sudbury, Massachusetts. Founded in 1716 as a "house of entertainment for travelers," it was already venerable in the nineteenth century when Henry Wadsworth Longfellow immortalized it in his *Tales of a Wayside Inn*. Restored by the Ford Foundation, Longfellow's Wayside Inn is the oldest inn still operating in the country, and both its charm and many of its recipes are cherished legacies from an earlier time.

Poached Salmon
Serves 3 to 4

1 quart water
1 cup dry white wine
1 tablespoon vinegar
1 carrot, sliced
1 large onion, sliced
1 celery stalk and leaves, sliced
2 sprigs parsley
1 bay leaf
6 peppercorns
2 teaspoons salt
3 to 4 salmon steaks

Combine all ingredients except salmon. Simmer slowly for 30 minutes; strain into a large skillet. Wrap each salmon steak in a piece of cheesecloth. Place in hot liquid. Cover. Cook over low heat until fish flakes easily, about 15 minutes. Remove cheesecloth. Serve hot or cold with Easy Mock Hollandaise sauce.

Easy Mock Hollandaise

1 can (10½ ounces) condensed cream of celery soup
1 tablespoon lemon juice
¼ cup mayonnaise

Left: Poached Salmon, Hollandaise

Blend ingredients. Heat slowly, stirring often. Serve with cooked vegetables or fish. Makes 1⅓ cups of sauce.

Wayside Inn Mushroom Sauce

¼ cup butter
½ teaspoon salt
Dash pepper
6 tablespoons flour
½ cup light cream
1 can (10½ ounces) condensed beef broth
or *chicken broth*
¾ cup water
3 tablespoons Burgundy wine
12 fresh mushrooms, 2 inches in diameter, sliced

Melt butter and stir in salt, pepper, and flour. Stir over low heat for 5 minutes, but do not brown. Stir in cream gradually until smooth. Stir in beef broth, water, and Burgundy. Cook, stirring, over low heat until sauce bubbles and thickens. Add mushrooms and simmer 5 minutes or until mushrooms are just cooked. Makes about 3½ cups of sauce. Serve over broiled filets mignons.

Adaptations from recipes by Chef Gino DiLuca.

Wayside Inn Shrimp Sauce

Serves 6

½ pound medium raw shrimp
1½ cups water
¼ cup butter
¼ cup flour
1 can (10½ ounces) condensed chicken broth
¾ cup shrimp cooking water
1 tablespoon lemon juice
2 egg yolks, slightly beaten
½ teaspoon salt
¼ teaspoon pepper

Combine shrimp and water in a saucepan. Bring to a boil; lower heat and simmer for 3 minutes. Drain and reserve ¾ cup of the cooking liquid. Shell and devein shrimp and cut into small pieces. Melt butter in a saucepan and stir in flour. Gradually stir in chicken broth, shrimp water, and lemon juice. Cook over low heat, stirring constantly, until sauce bubbles and thickens. Beat some of the hot sauce into the egg yolks. Beat this into remaining sauce. Season with salt and pepper. Add shrimp and stir to reheat, but do not boil. Spoon over servings of baked or broiled fish. Makes enough sauce for 6 servings halibut steak, haddock fillet, or fillet of sole.

Wayside Inn Chicken Pie

Serves 6

1 stewing chicken, about 4 or 5 pounds, cut up
2 cans (10½ ounces each) condensed chicken broth
2 soup cans water
¼ cup chopped parsley
1 cup sliced celery
1 carrot, sliced
1 medium onion, sliced
¼ teaspoon pepper
3 large onions, sliced
¼ cup butter
½ cup flour
1 cup light cream
3 cups broth reserved from chicken
1 package (10 ounces) frozen peas
Salt, pepper
1 package pie-crust mix

Combine chicken, chicken broth, water, parsley, celery, carrot, onion, and pepper in a large saucepan. Cover and simmer for 1 to 1½ hours or until chicken is tender. Drain chicken and reserve broth. Remove skin and bones from chicken and cut meat into large pieces. Sauté onions in a large skillet in butter. When onions are pale golden brown, stir in flour. Gradually stir in light cream and 3 cups of the broth drained from the chicken. Cook over low heat, stirring constantly, until sauce bubbles and thickens slightly. Stir in peas and chicken pieces. Season to taste. Pour mixture into a shallow, 2-quart casserole (10 x 10 x 2½ inches). Prepare pie crust according to package directions. Roll out large enough to fit the top of the casserole. Crimp edges and prick top with knife to allow steam to escape. Bake in a preheated 400°F. oven for 25 to 30 minutes or until crust is deeply browned.

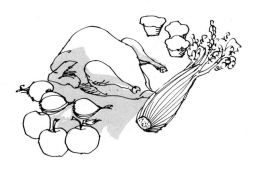

Roast Goose

Serves 8

1 goose, about 10 to 12 pounds (thaw if frozen)
Salt
¼ cup diced salt pork
⅓ cup diced bacon
1 cup finely chopped onion
4 cups diced peeled cooking apples
1 cup diced celery
1½ cups toasted bread cubes or packaged croutons
1½ cups finely crumbled corn muffins
Pepper
1 can (10½ ounces) condensed chicken broth

Sprinkle goose inside and out with salt. Render salt pork until pieces are brown. Remove salt pork pieces. Add bacon and fry until bacon is crisp. Add onion and sauté until onion is lightly browned. Stir in apples and celery and sauté another 5 minutes. Fold in bread cubes and corn muffins. Season to taste with pepper. Add chicken broth and stir to mix. Use mixture to stuff goose. Sew or skewer opening. Roast in a shallow pan on a rack in a preheated 350°F. oven for 3½ to 4 hours or until leg of goose is easily moved up and down and juices run yellow, not pink.

Hanalei Plantation

Hanalei Plantation in Kauai, Hawaii, offers the visitor a full day every day: sight-seeing, almost any sport that comes to mind, or just relaxing and being lazy— in short, there is something for everyone here. The resort is a complex of buildings on lovely Hanalei Bay. The vacationer may stay in the hotel itself or in one of a long row of cottages stretching from the swimming pool down to the bay. Within a short distance there is much breathtaking scenery, to be viewed by car or, in some cases, by helicopter. At the hotel there are skin diving, surfing, water skiing, swimming, fishing, shuffleboard, pitch-and-putt, and much more to entertain the visitor. If a whole day is to be spent out of doors, the hotel will supply a box lunch to be eaten beside one of the scenic trails nearby. "Hana" means *to make,* "lei" is a wreath of flowers or shells; "Hanalei" means *make a lei.* The Hanalei valley is called "birthplace of rainbows." All there is to see and do brings the visitor ravenous to the dining room. There he can feast on food as delicious as the surroundings are beautiful, from a menu international in scope. Crowning the evening are delightful performances of native singers and dancers, capturing visitors in the unfailing spell of exotic island magic.

Crêpes Dianne
Serves 4 to 6

2 tablespoons butter
½ cup chopped onion
¼ cup chopped parsley
1½ cups finely diced cooked turkey
1 can (10½ ounces) condensed cream of
mushroom soup
1 can (10 ounces) frozen condensed cream of shrimp
soup, thawed
12 crêpes (see index)
2 cups grated Swiss cheese

In a saucepan melt butter and sauté onion until tender. Remove from heat. Add parsley, turkey, and soups. Stir to blend. Spoon filling at one end of each crêpe. Roll up and place crêpes side by side in a greased shallow casserole. Sprinkle with Swiss cheese. Bake in a preheated 350°F. oven for 20 to 25 minutes or until crêpes are heated and cheese is golden brown.

Bloody Bullshot
Serves 7

1 can (10½ ounces) condensed beef broth
1 can (12 ounces) "V-8" juice
2 tablespoons Worcestershire sauce
½ teaspoon Tabasco sauce
Dash each salt, pepper, celery salt
Squeeze of lime
Vodka

Mix all except vodka in advance. When ready to serve, stir, pour over ice in 7 glasses. Add 2 ounces vodka to each glass. Garnish with celery sticks.

Adapted by Chef Toribio Bobby Pascua.

Look's "Sir=Loin"

Largest city of the South, Houston was named after Sam Houston, the first president of the Republic of Texas. Some fifty miles of waterway flowing into the Gulf of Mexico make Houston the third largest port in the United States. Present-day Houston is proud of its civic center, its Museum of Fine Arts, its unique stadium, the Astrodome, and its famous science and engineering school, Rice University. Houston diners-out flock to Look's "Sir-Loin" restaurants for fine food. Decorated in the English Tudor manner, these lavish steak houses commemorate a highlight of gastronomic history—the moment when Henry VIII, after a particularly rewarding feast which featured his favorite cut of beef, drew his sword and dubbed this choice cut "Sir Loin." Look's "Sir-Loin" serves many well-prepared dishes, but—in keeping with its name—makes a special point of fastidiously aged steaks, shipped as often as three times a week from Chicago, served with Look's famous bucket of crisp raw vegetables.

Golden Mushroom "Sir-Loin" Beef Tips

Serves 6

2 pounds beef, cut into 1-inch cubes
¼ cup butter or margarine
¾ cup sherry
1 medium clove garlic, minced
2 cans (10½ ounces each) condensed golden
mushroom soup
1 tablespoon finely chopped onion or shallots
½ cup water
Cooked noodles

In skillet, brown beef in butter. Add remaining ingredients. Cover and cook over low heat 2 hours or until tender. Stir now and then. Serve over noodles.

Tudie's Chicken Dinner

Serves 4

1 chicken, about 2 to 2½ pounds, cut up
Salt, pepper

Left: Golden Mushroom "Sir-Loin" Beef Tips

⅓ cup melted butter
1 can (10½ ounces) condensed cream of
celery soup
1 can (10½ ounces) condensed cream of
mushroom soup
½ cup dry white wine
3 cups cooked rice
¼ cup finely chopped parsley

Wash chicken and pat dry. Sprinkle pieces with salt and pepper. Brown chicken on all sides in butter. Pour off excess fat. Add soups and wine. Stir to blend. Cover and simmer for 40 to 45 minutes or until the chicken is tender. Place hot rice on a large platter, pour the chicken and gravy over rice. Garnish with chopped parsley. Serve the chicken with fruit salad or cranberry sauce and a green vegetable and dessert to complete the dinner.

Adapted by Chef Albert Evans and Mrs. Tudie Swink.

Heritage Hill Inn

Although it has been in operation little more than ten years, Heritage Hill Inn, in Holland, Massachusetts, fits admirably into the tradition of New England inns. It is housed in a lovely old home built in 1750. It is small—only six guest rooms—and it is noted for its gracious hospitality and its beautiful Colonial furnishings and decoration. The fireplace dominates the main dining room, where only authentic New England food is served. The Lusks are the owners; Mrs. Lusk does all the cooking.

Ham Pancakes

Serves 6, 2 crêpes each serving

Crêpes

½ cup all-purpose flour
1 teaspoon each, sugar, salt
2 tablespoons melted butter
¾ cup milk
3 egg yolks
3 egg whites, stiffly beaten

Filling

2 cups ground cooked or smoked ham
3 hard-cooked eggs, chopped
1 cup grated Swiss cheese
2 cans (10¾ ounces each) condensed Cheddar
cheese soup
½ cup light cream

Sift flour, sugar, and salt into a bowl. Add melted butter, milk, and egg yolks and beat until smooth. Fold in egg whites. Lightly grease a 6-inch skillet. Heat skillet and pour in about 2 tablespoons of the batter. Spread evenly over bottom of skillet. Cook until golden brown on each side. Repeat, using all batter. In a bowl, combine ham, hard-cooked eggs, ¾ cup of the grated cheese, and ½ cup of the Cheddar cheese soup. Spoon filling on pancakes and roll up. Place filled pancakes in a greased shallow baking pan. Combine remaining soup with cream; beat until smooth. Spoon over pancakes. Sprinkle top with remaining grated cheese. Bake in preheated 400°F. oven 20 minutes, until brown.

New England Steak and Kidney Pie

Serves 4

4 lamb kidneys
2 tablespoons oil
1½ pounds round steak
⅓ cup flour
1 can (10½ ounces) condensed onion soup
1½ tablespoons Worcestershire sauce
½ package pie-crust mix

Remove skin, fat, and muscle from kidneys; soak in cold water half an hour. Trim, dice fat from meat; render in a deep saucepan. Add oil. Cut kidneys and beef into ¾-inch cubes. Brown on all sides in hot fat. Sprinkle flour over meat, stir until mixture thickens. Stir in onion soup and Worcestershire sauce. Cover; simmer over very low heat until tender, 1 to 1½ hours. Stir occasionally to keep from sticking; add a little water if too thick. Pour meat mixture into a shallow 1-quart baking pan. Prepare pie-crust mix according to package directions; roll out to cover top of pan. Place crust over meat; crimp edges. Slash top to allow steam to escape. Bake in preheated 400°F. oven for 30 to 40 minutes or until browned.

Adaptations from recipes by Co-Owner Katherine G. Lusk.

Johnny and Kay's

Des Moines has been in turn a military garrison, the county seat, and the state capital. It is the heart of the Iowa farmland, a prairie metropolis. Here, in 1924, Johnny and Kay Compiano started a one-room restaurant. Today the little restaurant, Johnny and Kay's, has expanded to seven rooms and its frequently changed décor is as stimulating to the customer's eye as the outstanding food is to his appetite. Other professionals seeking the owners' recipes are matter-of-factly told that some of the popular dishes were developed "by mistake"—or, perhaps, "inspiration." This fine restaurant-hotel complex is now owned by the Hyatt Corporation of America.

Old-Fashioned Pot Roast

Serves 6

4 pounds beef shoulder pot roast
3 tablespoons rendered chicken fat
2 cloves garlic, minced
2 tablespoons salt
½ teaspoon paprika
4 bay leaves
10 peppercorns
1 can (10¾ ounces) condensed vegetable and
  beef stockpot soup
1 can (10½ ounces) condensed onion soup
2 tablespoons firmly packed brown sugar
¾ cup water
2 tablespoons flour mixed with ¼ cup water

In a Dutch oven, brown pot roast in chicken fat on all sides. Add garlic, salt, paprika, bay leaves, peppercorns, soups, brown sugar, and water. Cover; simmer for 2 to 2½ hours or until meat is tender. Remove meat; cut into slices. Stir flour mixture quickly into pan juices. Cook over low heat, stirring constantly until sauce thickens. Place pot roast slices in gravy; simmer 15 minutes. Serve with dumplings or noodles.

Sliced Veal Steaks Bombay

Serves 4

1½-pound leg of veal, cut ½ inch thick
½ clove garlic, mashed
Salt, pepper
Flour
3 tablespoons butter
1 large onion, sliced

Sauce

1 can (10¾ ounces) condensed tomato soup
1 teaspoon firmly packed brown sugar
1 teaspoon curry powder
1 teaspoon white wine
1 teaspoon soy sauce
1 can (1 pound) tomatoes, sliced, and their juice

Cut veal into 8 pieces, trimming meat. Rub meat with garlic. Sprinkle meat with salt and pepper. Dip meat into flour, coating slices completely. Melt butter in large skillet; brown meat and onions. Combine remaining ingredients; pour over meat. Cover; simmer, stirring occasionally, until the veal is tender, about 45 minutes.

Adapted by Chef Otis Fox.

Lüchow's

On May 1, 1882, the name Lüchow's went up over the doors of a restaurant on East Fourteenth Street in New York City, and founded a tradition that has survived more than eight decades of change. Fourteenth Street was then the heart of the city; the Academy of Music and Tony Pastor's stood cheek by jowl with Tiffany's and Tammany Hall. Nothing along the once-glittering thoroughfare is now as it was then—except for Lüchow's. The rooms that have been added to this fine old restaurant have only enhanced the dark-paneled Germanic atmosphere. There are still thirty-two kinds of beer and unique German wines; the menu is still long and lavish, with more than two hundred items from which to choose. The band still plays; there are still festivals to enjoy—Oktoberfest, Bock Beer, Venison, Goose, and May Wine Festivals, as well as many others. Lüchow's is still Lüchow's, for which each new generation of New Yorkers—and every visitor who knows his gustatory landmarks—gives thanks.

Sauerbraten

Serves 6 to 8

2 cans (10¾ ounces each) condensed old-fashioned
vegetable soup
1 cup red wine vinegar
1 tablespoon sugar
½ teaspoon pepper
4 whole cloves
4 peppercorns
2 bay leaves
3 pounds round steak
8 or 10 gingersnaps, crushed

In a large bowl, combine soup, vinegar, sugar, pepper, cloves, peppercorns, and bay leaves. Place beef in soup mixture. Cover; store in refrigerator 4 days. On fifth day, drain meat. Brown on all sides, add a little shortening if necessary. Add marinade liquid. Remove bay leaves. Cover. Cook over low heat about 3 hours or until tender. Remove meat to warm serving platter.

Left: Sauerbraten, Red Cabbage

Force broth through a wire strainer. Remove fat from gravy. Add gingersnaps; cook until thickened. Serve with meat. Use leftovers in Sauerbraten in Aspic.

Sauerbraten in Aspic

Serves 6 to 8

2 envelopes unflavored gelatin
2 cans (10½ ounces each) condensed beef broth or
consommé
1 cup Madeira wine
2 cups cooked, cubed Sauerbraten

In a saucepan, soften gelatin in 1 cup soup. Heat slowly to dissolve. Add remaining soup and wine. Chill until slightly thickened. Fold in Sauerbraten. Pour into 6-cup mold. Chill until firm. Serve on crisp salad greens. Garnish as desired. *Note:* Decorate bottom of mold with cut raw vegetables before adding gelatin mixture, if desired.

Adapted by Chef Jan Mitchell.

Hot Potato Salad with Bacon

Serves 6 to 8

4 pounds potatoes
12 slices bacon, diced
2 medium onions, diced
½ to 1 cup white vinegar, according to taste
1 can (10½ ounces) condensed chicken broth
½ teaspoon pepper
2 teaspoons sugar
2 egg yolks
Salt

Boil potatoes in their skins until tender but still firm. Cool, peel, and cut into ¼-inch slices. Cook bacon in a large skillet until crisp. Add onion and cook until transparent. Stir in vinegar, broth, pepper, and sugar. Beat egg yolks and stir quickly into mixture. Cook over low heat, stirring, until very hot but do not boil. Pour mixture over potato slices. Toss gently to blend. Serve hot. Season to taste with salt.

Hash à la Lubeck

Serves 6

3½ cups finely diced cold roast beef
2 teaspoons chopped capers
4 anchovies, minced
3 eggs, well beaten
¼ cup dry bread crumbs
¼ teaspoon pepper
1 teaspoon salt
¼ teaspoon grated nutmeg
1 package pie-crust mix
Caper Sauce

Combine beef, capers, anchovies, eggs, bread crumbs, pepper, salt, and nutmeg. Prepare pie-crust mix according to package directions. Roll out ⅔ of the pie crust large enough to line the bottom and sides of an 8-inch pie pan. Fill with beef mixture. Roll out remaining pie crust large enough to cover the top of the pie pan. Press edges together with the tines of a fork. Prick top. Cut flowers and leaves or other decorations from pie-crust trimmings. Brush top of pie with water and place decoration in an attractive pattern on top of pie. Bake in a preheated 350°F. oven for 45 minutes to 1 hour or until top is richly browned. Serve with Caper Sauce.

Caper Sauce

3 tablespoons butter
3 tablespoons flour
½ teaspoon Worcestershire sauce
1 can (10½ ounces) condensed beef broth
1 tablespoon capers
¾ cup water

Melt butter and stir in flour. Add Worcestershire sauce and gradually stir in beef broth, capers, and water. Cook over low heat, stirring constantly, until sauce bubbles and thickens. Makes about 2¼ cups of sauce.

Breast of Guinea Hen, Sous Cloche

Serves 4

2 cups wild rice
½ cup butter
2 small onions, chopped
2 cans (10½ ounces each) condensed chicken broth
Water
4 slices Virginia ham
⅓ cup butter
4 breasts of guinea hen
Salt, pepper
8 mushroom caps
4 slices toast
2 tablespoons flour
1 cup sherry
1 can (10½ ounces) condensed chicken broth

Wash rice and drain well. Melt ½ cup of butter and sauté onions until golden. Add 2 cans chicken broth and enough water to cover. Simmer, adding more water if necessary from time to time to prevent sticking. Cook until rice is tender and liquid is absorbed. Sauté ham in ⅓ cup of butter and set aside. Sprinkle guinea hen with salt and pepper. Sauté breasts in pan drippings until golden brown. Keep cooking slowly until breasts are tender, about 30 to 35 minutes. Sauté mushroom caps in butter with guinea hen. When guinea hen is tender place ham on toast; spoon wild rice over ham and top with guinea hen breast and mushrooms. Stir flour into pan drippings. Add sherry and 1 can chicken broth. Cook, stirring, until sauce bubbles and thickens. Spoon sauce over guinea hen. At Lüchow's this is served under glass—"sous cloche."

Fricassee of Chicken Giblets with Rice

Serves 6

1 pound chicken giblets
1 teaspoon salt
¼ teaspoon pepper
2 cans (10½ ounces each) condensed chicken broth
¾ cup water
2 carrots, diced
4 small onions, chopped
1 cup finely chopped celery
2 tablespoons butter
1 cup white wine
3 tablespoons flour

86

1 tablespoon lemon juice
2 egg yolks
½ cup heavy cream
2 cups cooked rice

Wash and drain giblets. Trim heavy muscles and cut into bite-size pieces. In a kettle combine giblets, salt, pepper, chicken broth, water, vegetables, butter, and white wine. Cover and simmer about 2 hours or until giblets are tender. Blend well flour, lemon juice, egg yolks, and heavy cream. Stir mixture into hot giblet mixture. (If desired, giblets may be strained to remove vegetables if you wish a smooth sauce.) Cook over low heat, stirring constantly, until sauce is hot. Do not boil. Fold in rice and serve at once.

Liver Dumplings

Serves 6 to 8 (24 dumplings)

½ pound lean fresh pork
½ pound kidney suet
1 pound calves' liver
1 onion, chopped
1 teaspoon butter
12 slices white bread, crusts removed
1 cup heavy cream
2 eggs, well beaten
1½ teaspoons salt
½ teaspoon pepper
¼ teaspoon grated nutmeg
1 clove garlic, mashed
1 cup flour (about)
3 cans (10½ ounces each) condensed beef broth
3 soup cans water
½ cup dry bread crumbs
¼ cup butter

Grind pork, suet, and liver coarsely. Sauté onion in 1 teaspoon butter until soft but not brown. Add to meat along with bread, cream, eggs, salt, pepper, nutmeg, garlic, and enough flour to make a stiff dough. Blend well, mashing mixture thoroughly. Combine soup and water in a large kettle. Bring to a boil; lower heat to simmering. Shape liver mixture into 24 balls, using lightly moistened hands. Drop into simmering soup and simmer 20 minutes. Remove from stock with a slotted spoon and place on a platter. Combine crumbs and ¼ cup butter and stir over low heat until crumbs are brown. Sprinkle crumbs over dumplings. Dumplings can also be served in the broth in which they were cooked for a hearty main dish soup.

Homemade Chicken Liver Pâté

¼ pound onions, diced
¼ cup chicken or goose fat

½ pound ground pork liver, diced
1 pound chicken livers
6 ounces salt pork, diced
1 can (10½ ounces) condensed chicken broth
⅛ teaspoon crumbled thyme
½ bay leaf, crumbled
1 egg, well beaten
¼ cup heavy cream
¼ cup sherry
2 tablespoons cornstarch

Sauté onions in fat until transparent and tender. Add livers, salt pork, chicken broth, thyme, and bay leaf. Cook at a simmer until liver is well done, about 40 minutes. Whirl liver and broth in a blender until smooth. Pour into a saucepan; stir in egg and cream. Mix sherry and cornstarch and stir into liver mixture. Cook over low heat, stirring, until mixture bubbles and thickens. Pour mixture into a 1-quart crock. Pour 2 tablespoons melted butter over the top, if desired, or cover closely with foil. Chill until firm. Use as a spread on slices of dark or rye bread. Makes about 3½ cups. *Variation:* Add 2 tablespoons minced anchovies or 2 tablespoons minced truffles to liver mixture.

Herring Appetizer

Serves 10 to 12

2 salt herrings
3 boiled potatoes, peeled and diced
2 sour apples, peeled and diced
2 dill pickles, diced
1 large cooked beet, shredded, or 1 can (8 ounces)
diced beets, drained
1 cup finely diced cooked veal
½ green pepper, diced
2 tablespoons minced onion
Dash black pepper
1 teaspoon sugar
¼ teaspoon dry mustard
¼ cup olive oil
½ cup wine vinegar
1 can (10½ ounces) condensed beef broth
Lettuce leaves
3 tablespoons drained capers
3 hard-cooked eggs, sliced

Rinse herring; cover with cold water and let soak overnight. Drain; remove skin and slice fillets from bones. Pull out all fine bones. Chop herring into ½-inch pieces. Combine herring with all ingredients except lettuce, capers, and eggs. Let stand in refrigerator overnight. Drain mixture well. Spoon herring salad on top of lettuce leaves. Sprinkle with capers and garnish with hard-cooked egg slices.

Mario's of Dallas

Mario's of Dallas is delightful because of its small-scaled, luxuriously intimate atmosphere in a part of the country that makes a point of having most things larger than life-size. In this treasure box lined with velvet the patron can still discuss the ways and means of a special dish, as he used to do in the restaurant's early days when Mario himself would take part in a tableside conference before retiring backstage into the kitchen to turn the diner's Lucullan dream into memorable reality.

Saltimbocca alla Romana
Veal with Ham and Cheese
Serves 4

*8 pieces boneless veal, 3 ounces each, pounded
until paper thin
Salt, pepper
Flour
⅓ cup butter
½ cup dry white wine
¼ cup "V-8" juice
1 can (10½ ounces) condensed chicken broth
2 tablespoons lemon juice
8 ounces Mozzarella cheese, cut into 8 slices
8 thin slices prosciutto ham*

Sprinkle veal with salt and pepper. Dust veal with flour. In a large skillet heat butter and brown veal slices on both sides. Remove veal and place pieces side by side in a greased shallow baking pan. Sprinkle 3 tablespoons flour into drippings in skillet. Gradually stir in wine,"V-8", chicken broth, and lemon juice. Cook over low heat, stirring constantly, until sauce thickens. Place 1 slice Mozzarella and 1 slice prosciutto over each veal cutlet. Bake in a preheated 375°F. oven for 10 minutes or until cheese melts. Place cutlets on a platter. Spoon hot sauce over meat. Garnish Saltimbocca with watercress sprigs.

Crab Meat Bel Paese
Serves 4

*½ medium onion, chopped
2 tablespoons butter
6 mushrooms, thinly sliced
1 pound lump crab meat, fresh or frozen
1 can (10½ ounces) condensed cream of
chicken soup
⅓ cup white wine
1 small avocado, peeled, seeded, and diced
½ cup grated provolone cheese
½ cup slivered almonds*

In a skillet sauté onions in butter until tender. Add mushrooms and sauté until mushrooms are wilted. Stir in crab meat, cream of chicken soup, and white wine. Simmer 5 minutes, stirring occasionally. Fold in avocado. Pour mixture into a 1½-quart casserole. Sprinkle top with cheese and almonds. Bake in a preheated 375°F. oven for 20 minutes, or until lightly browned and bubbly.

Left: Saltimbocca alla Romana

Adaptations from recipes by Manager Philip J. Vaccaro.

LONDON CHOP HOUSE

Those who know where to go in the business heart of Detroit will head for the London Chop House, an executives' oasis that serves hearty masculine food. The Gruber brothers, who own it, are also responsible for The Bull-Shot, a beef broth-and-vodka reviver for the weary that is now internationally famous.

Wild Duck Pancho

Serves 4

1 wild duckling, about 4 pounds
¼ cup celery leaves
½ cup coarsely chopped leeks
1 small red pepper pod
1 bay leaf
¼ pound salt pork, cut into ¼-inch-thick slices
2 tablespoons butter
2 tablespoons flour
1 can (10½ ounces) condensed beef broth
¼ cup orange juice
1 tablespoon currant jelly
2 tablespoons red wine
Salt, MSG

Stuff duckling with celery, leeks, pepper pod, and bay leaf. Place salt pork across the top of the duckling. Roast duckling on a rack in a shallow pan in a preheated 350°F. oven for 2½ hours or until leg bone moves up and down easily. Remove salt pork and stuffing from duck. Carve duckling and serve with sauce. *To prepare sauce:* melt butter, stir in flour. Gradually stir in beef broth, orange juice, jelly, and red wine. Cook over low heat, stirring constantly, until sauce bubbles and thickens. Season to taste with salt and MSG.

Adapted by Chef Philip Velez.

Moose Stew Chop House

Serves 6

2½ pounds moose meat, cut into 1-inch cubes
2 tablespoons shortening
¼ teaspoon cracked black pepper
½ teaspoon paprika
1 bay leaf
1 teaspoon salt
2 cans (10½ ounces each) condensed beef broth
1 cup dry red wine
1 large onion, diced
3 carrots, sliced
18 small whole white onions
12 small new potatoes, peeled
2 tablespoons butter
2 tablespoons flour

Sauté meat cubes in shortening until brown on all sides. Add pepper, paprika, bay leaf, salt, beef broth, red wine, onion, and carrots. Cover and simmer until meat is tender, about 2 hours. Add whole onions and potatoes; cover and simmer for an additional 15 minutes, or until the vegetables are barely tender. Mix butter and flour into a paste. Drop into simmering stew. Cook, stirring, until stew bubbles and thickens. Serve with rice or polenta.

Maitre Jacques

Maitre Jacques on the Charles offers gourmet French cuisine in a handsome contemporary setting. Overlooking Boston's Charles River, the restaurant's black-rimmed white china, white tablecloths, fine glassware, and fresh flowers set the scene for the delightful, individually prepared house specialties. Owner-Chef Lucien Robert learned his trade in the kitchens of Prunier and the Grand Hôtel in Paris.

Roulade Mornay

Crêpes with Seafood
Serves 6

¼ cup butter
2 shallots, diced, or 3 tablespoons minced
white onion
3 cups diced cooked fresh, frozen,
or canned lobster
½ pound bay scallops, cooked, diced
¾ pound medium shrimp, cooked, shelled,
deveined, diced
3 tablespoons Chablis wine
⅛ teaspoon each crumbled oregano, thyme
½ teaspoon salt
¼ teaspoon pepper
½ teaspoon prepared mustard
1 can (10½ ounces) condensed cream of
mushroom soup
12 crêpes (see index)
1 can (10½ ounces) condensed cream of
potato soup
¼ cup each grated Gruyère, Parmesan cheese

Melt butter in a large skillet. Sauté shallots until wilted but only pale yellow. Add lobster, scallops, shrimp, wine, oregano, thyme, salt, pepper, mustard, and mushroom soup; heat. Remove from heat and cool. Use mixture to fill crêpes. Place filled crêpes in a single layer in a greased shallow casserole. Combine remaining ingredients. Spread on top of crêpes. Bake in a preheated 400°F. oven 30 to 40 minutes, until bubbly.

Pintade* Sauce Smitane

Game Birds in Sour Cream Sauce
Serves 6

2 cans (10½ ounces each) condensed
chicken broth
3 Rock Cornish game hens
¼ cup butter
2 small white onions, minced
¼ cup Chablis wine
2 cups sour cream
Juice of 1 lemon

Heat chicken broth to boiling. Cut game hens in half and place in simmering broth. Cover; simmer until hens are just tender. Drain broth; reserve ⅓ cup for the sauce. Heat butter in a skillet; sauté onions until pale golden brown. Skin and bone the game hens; add to butter and onions. Add reserved chicken broth and wine. Stir in sour cream and lemon juice. Bring to a slow boil; simmer for 1 minute. Season to taste with salt. Serve over wild rice. (*European game for which there is no U.S. equivalent. Substitute Rock Cornish game hen.)

Adaptations from recipes by Chef Lucien Robert.

MAXIM'S de PARIS

Ever since it opened more than seventy years ago, Maxim's de Paris has been more than merely the restaurant at Number 3 Rue Royale. For generations of bon vivants it has been the spirit of Paris itself, where wit and wickedness and gaiety, fashion and flair, talent and brilliance added savor to the subtle delights of French cooking at its best. All of this ambience now glitters in an American branch of Maxim's in Chicago's Astor Tower Hotel. Every detail of the original has been re-created with astonishing fidelity and success: the carved mahogany and rich red velvet; the legendary cut-glass mirrors in which Gigi once admired herself; the magical glow of the pink-shaded table lamps that always turned every woman they illuminated into a beauty—at least for the night. And, of course, the menu and wines duplicate the glories of old Maxim's. Here, feasting on dishes that have delighted the most educated palates in the world, space-age Americans can forget the steel and cement outside, and recapture, however briefly, the sparkle and excitement of a time long gone by.

Veal Normande
Serves 4 to 6

1½ pounds veal cutlet
3 tablespoons butter or *margarine*
3 tablespoons brandy
1 can (10½ ounces) condensed cream of
mushroom soup
⅔ cup milk
1 apple, peeled and thickly sliced

Pound veal with meat hammer or edge of heavy saucer. In large skillet, brown veal in butter; remove from pan. Add brandy; stir to loosen browned bits. Stir in soup and milk. Add veal and apple; cook over low heat until tender, stirring now and then. Serve with rice.

Scallops à la Crevette
Serves 3

1 pound fresh bay scallops
¼ cup chopped onion
2 tablespoons butter or *margarine*
1 can (10 ounces) frozen condensed cream of shrimp
soup, thawed
¼ cup light cream
¼ cup vermouth
Buttered bread crumbs or *grated Cheddar cheese*

In a skillet, brown scallops and cook onion in butter until tender. Add soup, cream, and vermouth. Cook a few minutes to blend flavors. Spoon into individual ramekins. Top with buttered bread crumbs or grated cheese, if desired. Broil until top is brown.

Left: Veal Normande

Adaptations from recipes by Chef Pierre Rosi.

LA MEDITERRANEE

New and beautiful, the Hotel Pontchartrain is a part of Detroit's handsome new Civic Center. The Center is a group of buildings clustered in a dramatic setting on seventy-five waterfront acres along the Detroit River—a glamorous area very unlike the first-time visitor's notion of how this busy city will look. The hotel is opposite Cobo Hall, the convention center, and overlooks the river. One of the Pontchartrain's three restaurants is La Mediterranee, opened in 1965. The menu and décor of this charming dining place reflect the elegance of Continental Europe. Mirrored walls and blue and beige furnishings are complemented by the graceful brick arches and columns. Pink table linens and wrought-iron chandeliers lend festive notes, and fresh flowers on each table complete the gracious atmosphere. The menu is varied, offering the diner an unusual list of choices from which to compose an outstanding meal.

95

Soufflé au Fromage
Sauce aux Huîtres, Chez Moi

Cheese Soufflé with Oyster Sauce

Serves 4

½ cup boiling water
¼ cup butter or margarine
½ cup all-purpose flour
2 eggs
1 can (10¾ ounces) condensed Cheddar cheese soup
½ teaspoon salt
¼ teaspoon each pepper, nutmeg
½ clove garlic, minced
6 egg whites, stiffly beaten

Add butter to boiling water and stir until melted. Add flour, stirring over medium heat until mixture forms a ball. Remove from heat and add one egg at a time, beating until smooth after each addition. Stir in soup, salt, pepper, nutmeg, and garlic. Cool. Fold in egg whites. Pour mixture into a buttered and floured 2-quart soufflé dish. Bake in a preheated 375°F. oven for 25 to 30 minutes or until soufflé is puffed and golden brown. Serve at once with Sauce aux Huîtres, Chez Moi.

Sauce aux Huîtres, Chez Moi

2 tablespoons butter
2 tablespoons chopped onion
1 can (10 ounces) frozen condensed
oyster stew, thawed
1 tablespoon cornstarch
¼ cup dry sherry

Melt butter and sauté onion until tender but not brown. Stir in oyster stew. Mix cornstarch and sherry until smooth and stir mixture into oyster stew. Cook over low heat, stirring constantly, until sauce bubbles and thickens. Serve with Soufflé au Fromage. Makes about 1½ cups of sauce.

Left: Soufflé au Fromage, Sauce aux Huîtres

Adapted by Chef Larry Pagliara.

Marzetti's

It is not by accident that Columbus is the capital of Ohio. It was conceived, designed, and surveyed as a capital city. And with its broad, tree-lined streets, its Greek Revival Capitol building, Ohio State University, and the attractive arched bridges that span the Scioto River, it is a suitably handsome one. The city was planned in 1812, and construction began shortly afterward; by 1816 the Capitol, located in a lovely ten-acre park, was ready for the convening of the legislature. The National Road reached Columbus, bringing extensive stagecoach travel to the city; by 1850 travelers were able to use the new railroad, and the city's expansion was rapid. Although industry plays an important part in the life of present-day Columbus, government and education remain the city's primary functions. One of the oldest restaurants in the city—indeed, in the Midwest—is Marzetti's, still under the management of the Marzetti family, who came to Columbus in 1896 from Barga, near Florence, Italy. Marzetti's is famed for its authentic Italian dishes—pasta in great variety with many delicious sauces, risottos and salad dressings—and popular American dishes as well.

Ham and Hard-Cooked Eggs au Gratin

Serves 4

*1 can (10¾ ounces) condensed
Cheddar cheese soup
½ can (10½-ounce size) condensed cream of
celery soup
½ cup light cream
½ cup ground cooked, smoked, or boiled ham
¼ cup melted butter
8 hard-cooked eggs, sliced
½ cup cracker crumbs*

In a saucepan combine cheese soup, celery soup, cream, ham, and half of the butter. Heat until bubbly. Place 2 sliced eggs into each of 4 individual buttered casseroles. Spoon the hot sauce over the sliced eggs. Combine cracker crumbs and remaining melted butter, and spoon mixture over the sliced eggs and sauce.

Place under broiler and broil until bubbly and golden. *Note:* These casseroles may be prepared ahead of time and refrigerated. In that case, do not broil, but bake in a preheated 400°F. oven for 15 to 20 minutes or until casserole is bubbly and brown.

Cocktail Canapés

*1 can (10½ ounces) condensed cream of
celery soup
1 package (8 ounces) cream cheese
1 cup chopped or ground pepperoni*

Combine all ingredients and blend well. Spread on slices of party rye bread. Place under broiler until bubbly. Serve immediately. Makes about 2½ cups of canapé spread.

Adapted by Owner Gertrude Marzetti Brown and Darlene Lindsay.

THE NATIONS INTERNATIONAL RESTAURANT

Norfolk, Virginia, dating from 1688, comprises with her sister city, Portsmouth, the oldest naval facility in the United States, and serves as home port for the Atlantic Fleet. A modern-day landmark in the lovely old city is The Nations, with its handsome décor, fine wines, and an international menu. Its maître d'hôtel, Tommy Seay, specializes in tableside drama, with emphasis on flambées and crêpes suzette.

Roast Boneless Chicken à la Louisiana

Serves 4

2 broiler-fryer chickens, about 1½ pounds each
Salt, paprika
12 fresh mushrooms, chopped
1 clove garlic, finely chopped
1 tablespoon finely chopped chives
3 tablespoons butter
1 can (10½ ounces) condensed consommé
⅓ cup white wine
1 package (9 ounces) frozen artichoke hearts
2 tablespoons cornstarch
¼ cup water
Salt, pepper

Sprinkle chicken inside and out with salt and paprika. Roast in a preheated 325°F. oven for 1 hour or until tender. Cool. Remove chicken from bones in large pieces and set aside. Sauté mushrooms, garlic, and chives in butter until wilted. Add consommé, white wine, and artichoke hearts; simmer until artichokes are tender. Mix cornstarch and water and stir quickly into sauce. Cook over low heat, stirring constantly, until sauce bubbles and thickens. Season to taste with salt and pepper. Add chicken and spoon sauce over pieces, heating until sauce begins to bubble again. Serve while piping hot.

Steak Marcia

Serves 6

6 strip or shell steaks
1 can (10½ ounces) condensed consommé
1 clove garlic, minced
3 tablespoons A-1 sauce
3 tablespoons oil
2 tablespoons honey
½ cup red wine
½ teaspoon salt
1 tablespoon cornstarch
¼ cup water

Place steaks in a shallow glass or enamel pan. Add remaining ingredients except cornstarch and water. Marinate for 2 hours at room temperature. Drain steaks and reserve marinade. Broil steaks to desired doneness. In a saucepan combine cornstarch and water. Gradually stir in reserved marinade. Cook over low heat, stirring constantly, until sauce bubbles and thickens. Serve over hot broiled steaks.

Adaptations from recipes by Manager Tommy Seay.

Northstar Inn

The Northstar Inn is an outstanding restaurant in a city—Minneapolis—where good eating has been a cherished tradition for generations. But it presents a built-in problem to those who are merely passing through town. Situated on the seventh floor of the Northstar Center, one of the city's biggest and busiest office buildings, the Inn fills up so quickly with regulars from neighboring floors that transients must reserve well in advance for a chance to sample the fine internationally flavored cuisine.

Beef Wellington

Serves 4

¼ cup butter
4 beef tenderloin filets, 4 ounces each
Salt, pepper
1 clove garlic, crushed
½ cup chopped fresh mushrooms
1 small onion, minced
6 mushrooms, sliced
3 tablespoons flour
½ cup red wine
1 can (10½ ounces) condensed beef broth
1 bay leaf
Worcestershire sauce
1 can (4 ounces) liver pâté
1 package pie-crust mix (enough for 2 crusts)
¼ cup butter
Cold water
1 egg, beaten

Melt butter in a skillet. Sprinkle filets with salt, pepper, and rub with garlic. Sauté steaks in butter 3 to 4 minutes on each side. Drain steaks; chill. To pan drippings add chopped mushrooms; sauté until wilted. Remove mushrooms with a slotted spoon, draining carefully, and chill. Add onion and sliced mushrooms to pan drippings. When mushrooms are wilted, stir in flour. Gradually stir in red wine and beef broth. Add bay leaf and cook, stirring, until sauce bubbles and thickens. Season to taste with salt, pepper, and Worcestershire. Mix chilled chopped mushrooms with liver pâté. Spread mixture like frosting over the tops of the chilled steaks. Refrigerate. Prepare pie crust as directed on package, cutting in ¼ cup butter until particles are very fine before adding cold water. Roll out pie crust and cut into 4 6-inch squares. Save pie-crust trimmings for decorations. Brush squares of pie crust with beaten egg. Place steaks, pâté-spread side down, on the pie crust. Fold dough over the steak enclosing it completely and sealing the edges with beaten egg. Place steaks seam side down on a greased cookie sheet. Brush tops with beaten egg. Cut scraps of dough with scissors and make desired design on top. Brush design with beaten egg. Bake in a preheated 425°F. oven for 15 to 20 minutes or until crust is richly browned. Serve hot with hot sauce. *Note:* The Wellingtons may be prepared up to four days in advance, and refrigerated. They may also be frozen and stored for up to a month, but should be thawed before baking.

Left: Beef Wellington

Adapted by Chef Hans Gitgen.

Arroz con Pollo Valencia

Chicken with Rice, Valencia Style
Serves 6

1 chicken, about 3 pounds, cut into serving pieces
2 tablespoons olive oil
1 medium onion, chopped
1 medium green pepper, diced
6 mushrooms, quartered
2 cans (10½ ounces each) condensed chicken broth
1½ cups converted rice
2 cloves garlic, chopped
1 package saffron (1 teaspoon crumbled threads)
2 tomatoes, chopped
1 tablespoon chopped chives (optional)
½ teaspoon oregano
2 bay leaves
Pinch thyme (optional)
Pinch rosemary (optional)
1 cup white wine
¼ cup chopped pimiento
1 package (10 ounces) frozen peas
12 stuffed olives, sliced
½ pound raw jumbo shrimp, shelled and deveined
2 South African rock lobster tails, 4 ounces each, cut,
shell and all, into 4 crosswise pieces
12 littleneck clams, scrubbed
1 jar (2¾ ounces) Danish shrimp, drained

Brown chicken on all sides in olive oil in a large kettle.
Add onion, green pepper, and mushrooms. Sauté
until vegetables are wilted. Add chicken broth, rice,
garlic, saffron, tomatoes, chives, oregano, bay leaves,
thyme, rosemary, and white wine. Cover and simmer,
stirring occasionally, until rice is tender and liquid is
almost absorbed. Add remaining ingredients. Cover
and simmer for 10 to 15 minutes or until seafood is
cooked and clamshells have opened. Remove bay
leaves. Season to taste with salt. Serve hot. *Note:* If
littleneck clams are unavailable, use 1 can clams.

Venison Steak Mirza

Serves 6

3 pounds venison steak, about 1 inch thick
Salt, pepper, paprika
1 tablespoon crumbled rosemary
Flour
6 tablespoons butter
2 cups dry red wine
Water
1 can (10½ ounces) condensed golden
mushroom soup

Sprinkle steaks on both sides with salt, pepper, and
paprika. Rub with rosemary. Dip steaks into flour
to coat lightly. Melt butter in a large skillet and brown
steaks on both sides. Add wine; cover and simmer for
1½ to 2 hours, or until steaks are tender. Add small
amounts of water from time to time to prevent sticking.
Remove steaks to a platter. Stir soup into pan drippings
and reheat until bubbly. Spoon hot sauce over steaks.
Serve with baked apple, cranberry sauce, and noodles.

Roast Veal Paysanne

Serves 6

3 pounds boneless veal leg
3 slices lean bacon, cut into long strips
¼ cup diced salt pork
¼ cup butter
Flour
2 tablespoons chopped parsley
1 bay leaf
¼ teaspoon crumbled thyme
1 can (10¾ ounces) condensed old-fashioned
vegetable soup
1 cup dry white wine
1½ cups sour cream
Salt, pepper

Lard the veal with thin strips of bacon, using a larding
needle or knitting needle. Combine salt pork and
butter and fry until salt pork is golden brown. Roll
veal in flour; brown on all sides. Add parsley, bay
leaf, thyme, soup, and white wine. Cover and bake in
a preheated 350°F. oven for 1½ to 2 hours or until
meat is tender. Remove meat to a platter; keep warm.
Stir sour cream into pan drippings. Strain sauce; reheat only until hot—do not boil. Season to taste with
salt and pepper. Spoon sauce over slices of veal. Serve
with rice pilaf.

NENDEL'S

Portland, Oregon's largest city, stretches along both banks of the Willamette River. Within easy reach of the city are the Columbia River Gorge and Mount Hood, as well as numerous recreation areas set in some of the most breathtaking scenery the country has to offer. A celebrated annual ten-day rose festival, and the gardening efforts of its citizens, support Portland's claim to its title, "City of Roses." The oldest restaurant in continuous operation in Portland is Nendel's, which was started more than forty years ago as a luncheon place for the friends of the owner. Five pleasantly landscaped acres make a restful setting for the restaurant, whose main dining room now seats more than 150. Present owners are the Harringtons. Mrs. Harrington is hostess; Mr. Harrington supervises the kitchen, from which emerges good, old-fashioned, home-style food—in keeping with the Early American décor.

Chicken Araat

Serves 4

1 chicken, about 3 pounds, quartered
Salt, pepper
Flour
¼ cup butter
½ cup chopped onions
1 cup small, stemmed button mushrooms
1 can (10½ ounces) condensed chicken broth
½ cup sherry
3 tablespoons flour
½ cup heavy cream

Sprinkle chicken with salt and pepper. Dip pieces into flour and shake off excess. Fry chicken in butter until golden brown on all sides. Remove chicken and add onions and mushrooms. Brown until golden. Add chicken pieces, chicken broth, and sherry. Cover and simmer until chicken is tender, about 40 to 45 minutes. Remove chicken pieces and place on a bed of rice pilaf. Mix flour and cream. Stir flour mixture into pan drippings. Cook over low heat, stirring constantly, until sauce bubbles and thickens. Spoon sauce over chicken pieces and pilaf.

French Onion Soup

Serves 6

6 large yellow onions, thinly sliced
½ cup butter
2 cans (10½ ounces each) condensed beef broth
1 soup can water
1 soup can dry white wine
6 slices toasted French bread, about 1 inch thick
¾ cup grated Parmesan and Gruyère cheese (freshly grated if possible)

Sauté onions in butter until lightly browned. Add broth, water, and wine. Simmer until onions are tender. Spoon soup into earthenware or other ovenproof bowl. Top each serving with toasted French bread. Sprinkle with grated Parmesan and Gruyère cheese. Broil until cheese is melted and golden brown.

Adapted by Owner Robert Harrington.

Orléans Room

Omaha, Nebraska, was named for the Indians who once occupied the land on which the city is now situated. The Indians lived there until 1854, when they signed a treaty with the federal government, ceding the site. As soon as the treaty was official, new settlers, who had been waiting just across the river in Council Bluffs, Iowa, swept into the area. They brought with them all the trademarks of a land-rush boom—on the good side, new families and a growing population; on the bad side, gunfights in the streets, and fortunes lost in gambling houses. Omaha has changed since those early days; now it is the largest livestock market and meat-packing center in the world, a great commercial and industrial city. One of the hubs of this activity is the Blackstone Hotel, with its Orléans Room. Beef, not surprisingly, is a feature of the menu. Especially popular are the serve-yourself Sunday brunch and evening buffet.

Crêpes à la Reine

Serves 12

Crêpes
1½ cups flour
2 cups milk
4 eggs
2 tablespoons sugar
½ teaspoon salt
Butter or margarine

In bowl beat flour, milk, eggs, sugar, and salt until smooth. Chill 1 hour. In hot, greased small skillet, cook 24 crêpes (6 inches in diameter) on both sides, using 2 tablespoons batter for each.

Filling
1 can (10½ ounces) condensed cream of
chicken soup
1 can (10½ ounces) condensed cream of
mushroom soup
¼ cup light cream
½ cup sherry
4 cups diced cooked chicken

In a saucepan, blend soups until smooth; stir in cream, sherry, and chicken. Heat, stirring now and then. Fill each crêpe with 2 tablespoons chicken mixture and roll up. Place 2 filled pancakes on each plate; spoon additional filling at open ends.

Fillet of Sole Marguery

Serves 6

1 cup sliced mushrooms, about 4 ounces
4 tablespoons butter or margarine
1 can (10 ounces) frozen condensed cream of
shrimp soup
¼ cup Sauternes or other dry white wine
2 pounds fillet of sole
Paprika

In saucepan, cook mushrooms in butter; stir in soup and wine. Heat until soup thaws, stirring now and then. Place fillets in a shallow baking dish or broiler pan (without rack). Pour sauce over fish; sprinkle with paprika. Broil 10 minutes or until done.

Left: Crêpes à la Reine

Adapted by Chef Robert Barnett.

OLD STONE INN

Simpsonville lies between Lexington and Louisville, Kentucky—the heart of the fabulously beautiful bluegrass country, characterized by white-fenced pastures that are as elegantly manicured as the best of parks. Here the aristocracy of horse breeders lives and raises some of the world's prize horseflesh. Many of the stock farms are open to the public, and the thoroughbreds are well worth seeing. The visitor to this region will find a tempting luncheon or dinner at the Old Stone Inn, in Simpsonville, a handsome house built before the Civil War and once a rest station for stagecoach travelers. Decorated in Early American style, the Inn is still more like a home than a restaurant. The Old Stone Inn serves superb food in keeping with the spirit of its décor. The restaurant is open seven months a year—from April through October.

105

Scalloped Zucchini

Serves 6

4 large zucchini, cut into round slices ½ inch wide
4 hard-cooked eggs, chopped
1 can (10¾ ounces) condensed Cheddar cheese soup
⅓ cup heavy cream
½ cup grated sharp Cheddar cheese
¼ cup flavored dry bread crumbs

Layer zucchini and eggs alternately in a greased 8-inch square pan. The top layer should be eggs. Mix soup and cream; spoon evenly over casserole. Sprinkle top with cheese and bread crumbs. Bake in a preheated 350°F. oven for 40 to 45 minutes, or until zucchini is easily pierced with a fork and the top of the casserole is lightly browned.

Stuffed Eggplant

Serves 4

1 large eggplant
½ cup water
½ teaspoon salt
¼ cup chopped onion
1 tablespoon butter
1 can (10½ ounces) condensed cream of
mushroom soup
1 teaspoon Worcestershire sauce
1 cup fine butter-type cracker crumbs (about 24)
1 tablespoon chopped parsley
1½ cups water

Slice off one side of eggplant. Remove pulp to within ½ inch of skin. Dice removed pulp and place in saucepan. Add water and salt. Simmer until eggplant is tender. Drain. Sauté onion in butter until golden brown. Stir onion, mushroom soup, Worcestershire sauce, and all of the cracker crumbs except 2 tablespoons into eggplant pulp. Fill eggplant shell with mixture. Place eggplant in a shallow baking pan. Sprinkle top with reserved crumbs and parsley. Pour water into baking pan. Bake in a preheated 375° F. oven for 1 hour or until piping hot.

Left: Scalloped Zucchini, Stuffed Eggplant

Adapted by Sarah Tinsley.

Omar Khayyam's Restaurant

Generations of readers have been charmed by the romantic claim of the poet Omar Khayyam that a loaf of bread and a jug of wine—plus love—were all he wanted in life. Happily for the more prosaic, the restaurant in San Francisco that bears his name offers a far more lavish choice. Omar Khayyam's is basically an Armenian restaurant. Each meal begins with the lavash—traditional bread-breaking ceremony—and ends with such glorious confections as paklava, fifty-six feathery layers of pastry filled with ground walnuts and honey. Omar himself could not have been proof against such temptation—and neither are the delighted diners who return again and again.

Arkayagan Abour

Meatball Soup

Serves 6

½ pound lean venison or lamb, ground twice
½ cup cooked rice, ground wheat or bulghour
¼ cup finely chopped onion
¼ cup finely chopped parsley
2 cans (10½ ounces each) condensed chicken broth
2 soup cans water
⅓ cup lemon juice
2 eggs
Salt, pepper

Combine first four ingredients. Shape into ¾-inch balls. Heat broth and water to the simmering point. Add meatballs; simmer 15 to 20 minutes. In a soup tureen, beat lemon juice and eggs until smooth. Gradually beat in hot broth. Add meatballs last. Season to taste with salt, pepper.

Roast Veal with Sage Dressing

Serves 6

3 pounds boneless veal roast
Salt, pepper
1 onion, chopped
1 carrot, chopped
1 cup "V-8" juice
¼ cup flour
2 tablespoons butter
1 can (10½ ounces) condensed chicken broth
8 slices white bread, toasted and diced
1 can (10½ ounces) condensed onion soup
1 teaspoon crumbled sage
¼ teaspoon pepper
2 tablespoons melted butter
2 eggs, well beaten

Season roast with salt and pepper. Place in shallow roasting pan with onion, carrot, "V-8." Roast in a preheated 350° F. oven for 3 hours or until brown and tender. Keep warm on a platter. Drain and strain pan juices. For sauce, combine flour and butter in a saucepan; gradually stir in strained pan juices and chicken broth; cook, stirring, until sauce bubbles and thickens. For dressing, combine remaining ingredients and place in a shallow, greased 1-quart casserole. Roast with meat for additional 30 minutes. Slice meat and serve on dressing. Top with hot sauce.

Left: Arkayagan Abour

Adaptations from recipes by Owner George Mardikian.

Havabour

Lemon Soup
Serves 6

2 cans (10½ ounces each) condensed chicken broth
2 soup cans water
1 cup raw vermicelli, broken into 3-inch lengths
3 eggs, well beaten
½ cup lemon juice
Salt, pepper

In a large saucepan combine chicken broth and water. Bring to a boil; add vermicelli and cook until vermicelli is tender. Beat eggs with lemon juice. Gradually beat in some of the hot soup. Beat this mixture into the remaining soup. Reheat but do not boil. Season to taste with salt and pepper.

Lentils Sauté

Serves 8 to 10

1 package (1 pound) lentils
2 cans (10½ ounces each) condensed onion soup
3 cups water
½ cup olive oil
2 teaspoons salt
½ teaspoon pepper
2 tablespoons finely chopped parsley

Wash lentils and drain. Combine all ingredients in a large saucepan and simmer uncovered for 1 hour or until lentils are tender and liquid is almost absorbed. Serve lentils hot or cold.

Misov Spannak

Spinach Stew
Serves 4

1 pound tender shoulder of lamb
Salt, pepper
¼ cup butter
1 can (10½ ounces) condensed onion soup
1 cup "V-8" juice
2 pounds spinach, trimmed, washed, and coarsely torn into large pieces

Cut meat into 1-inch cubes. Sprinkle meat with salt and pepper. Brown meat on all sides in butter. Add onion soup, "V-8", and spinach. Cover and cook until lamb is tender, about 1 hour. Serve with chunks of bread for dunking in the pan juices.

108

Shish Kebab

Serves 6

1 leg of lamb, 5 to 6 pounds
2 cans (10½ ounces each) condensed onion soup
½ teaspoon freshly ground black pepper
⅔ cup sherry
¼ cup oil
1 teaspoon crumbled oregano

Remove meat from leg of lamb. Remove fat, gristle, and tendons. Cut meat into 1-inch cubes. Place cubes in a shallow pan. Combine remaining ingredients and pour over meat. Let stand at room temperature for 2 hours. Drain, reserving marinade. Thread meat on 6 long skewers. Broil 10 minutes on each side, brushing meat with marinade every 5 minutes. If broiling over charcoal, place skewers on a rack 6 inches above gray coals and broil 10 minutes on each side, brushing with marinade every 5 minutes. Serve hot with pilaff.

Zodiac

There are still a few cow towns in Texas. But it has been a long time since Dallas resembled them. Money, proliferating industry, and the whole forward thrust of the Texas boom have turned this erstwhile trading post into one of the most cosmopolitan cities in the nation—perhaps in the world. Its celebrated specialty store, Neiman-Marcus, dresses many of the women who pace international fashion—and it also sells planes, six-figure emerald necklaces, and Chinese junks sight unseen through the mail as matter-of-factly as Sears Roebuck sells washing machines. Understandably, The Zodiac restaurant too is something special—a rendezvous whose atmosphere and food are designed for a clientele that has set newly high standards for the good life—which include, of course, very high standards indeed for food excellently prepared and beautifully served. The menu offers many choices, usually including a zesty curry.

Curry of Lamb
Serves 4

¼ cup butter
¾ cup finely chopped onions
2 tablespoons finely chopped crystallized
or preserved ginger
2 teaspoons finely chopped fresh mint
1 tablespoon curry powder
1 can (10½ ounces) condensed cream of chicken soup
½ cup grated fresh coconut
1 tablespoon lime juice
½ cup heavy cream
3 cups diced cooked lamb

In a saucepan, melt butter and sauté onions until golden and tender. Add ginger, mint, curry, soup, coconut, lime juice, and heavy cream. Simmer for 5 minutes, stirring constantly. Stir in lamb and reheat until just bubbly. Spoon curry over hot cooked rice. Serve with chutney and other curry accompaniments. *Note:* If a spicier sauce is desired, increase curry powder to 2 tablespoons.

Beef à la Deutsch
Serves 6

2 tablespoons butter
½ cup sliced fresh mushrooms
¼ cup sliced green pepper
1½ pounds beef tenderloin, cut into
¼-inch-thick slices
2 tablespoons flour
1 can (10½ ounces) condensed onion soup
1½ cups sour cream
3 tablespoons diced pimiento

Melt butter and sauté mushrooms and green pepper until tender. Remove vegetables and brown meat slices in drippings. Add vegetables and sprinkle with flour. Stir in onion soup. Cook, stirring, until soup bubbles. Stir in sour cream and pimiento. Reheat but do not boil. Serve spooned over hot cooked green noodles.

Adaptations from recipes by Helen L. Corbitt.

Pirates' House

There is a tale that on moonless nights a voice echoes through the Pirates' House, hoarsely demanding, "Darby, bring the rum!" Any reader of Stevenson's *Treasure Island* will recognize these as the last words of Cap'n Flint, who is supposed to have expired in an upstairs room of this historic Savannah, Georgia, landmark, built in 1753. Flint's ghost is not the only one that haunts the seventeen dining rooms of the Pirates' House. The aura still remains of hard-eyed, ruthless pirates, and all the seafaring riffraff that came up the Savannah River in the days of "wooden ships and iron men." Shades of shanghaied sailors allegedly still wander in eternal misery through the old Rum Cellar. The Pirates' House is an accredited museum—and a museum that offers ghosts along with excellent food, beautifully served, is not the sort of thing one comes upon every day in every corner of the world.

Ham Buffet Mold

Serves 8 to 10

1 can (10¾ ounces) condensed tomato soup
¾ cup water
2 envelopes unflavored gelatin
½ cup cold water
1 package (3 ounces) cream cheese
2 tablespoons lemon juice
1 tablespoon grated onion
½ cup mayonnaise
2 teaspoons prepared mustard
2 cups finely chopped boiled or smoked ham

Combine soup and ¾ cup water and bring to a boil. Soak gelatin in ½ cup cold water for 5 minutes. Stir softened gelatin into hot soup. Add cream cheese and beat until smooth. Cool until slightly thickened. Stir in remaining ingredients. Pour mixture into a lightly oiled 6-cup mold. Chill for 4 hours or until the mold is firm. To unmold, dip mold into lukewarm water for a few seconds, tap to loosen and invert on a platter. Garnish with a variety of salad greens, hard-cooked egg slices, and stuffed olives.

Porcupine Meatballs

Serves 6

1 cup raw converted rice
1 pound ground round steak
¼ cup minced onions
1 teaspoon salt
½ teaspoon black pepper
2 cans (10¾ ounces each) condensed tomato soup

Mix rice, ground round, onions, salt, and pepper. Shape mixture into 24 1-inch balls. Drop balls into boiling water to cover. Simmer over low heat for 1 hour or until rice is tender and meatballs are easily pierced. By this time almost all the water will have been absorbed and some of the rice will be cooking in the liquid remaining. Add soup and stir very gently to blend. Reheat until bubbly.

Adapted by Owner Herb Traub.

Left: Ham Buffet Mold

Miss Edna's Seafood Bisque

Serves 6

1 can (11¼ ounces) condensed green pea soup
1 can (10¾ ounces) condensed tomato soup
1½ cups milk mixed with 1½ cups light cream
½ cup sherry
1 cup flaked crab meat
Lemon peel

Combine soups. Gradually stir in milk and cream. Cook over low heat, stirring occasionally, until soup bubbles. Stir in sherry and crab meat. Reheat slightly. Add a twist of lemon peel to each bowl of soup.

Asparagus and Egg Casserole

Serves 4

1 can (10¾ ounces) condensed Cheddar cheese soup
¼ cup milk
1 can (10 ounces) asparagus spears, drained
4 hard-cooked eggs, sliced
¼ cup toasted slivered almonds

Blend soup and milk. In 1-quart casserole, arrange alternate layers of asparagus, cheese sauce, eggs, and almonds. Bake at 375°F. for 20 minutes.

112

Ham Pie with Cheese Biscuit Topping

Serves 6

2 cans (10½ ounces each) condensed cream of celery soup
⅔ cup light cream
4 cups diced cooked ham
3 cups biscuit mix
1½ cups grated Cheddar cheese
1 cup milk

Combine soup, cream, and ham. Divide mixture equally among 6 individual casseroles of 1-cup capacity each. Combine biscuit mix and cheese. Toss to blend. Stir in milk and mix until dough cleans the bowl. Knead dough a few times on a lightly floured board until smooth. Roll out dough to ½-inch thickness and cut into rounds large enough to cover the tops of the casseroles. Bake in a preheated 350°F. oven for 30 minutes or until filling is bubbly and crust is brown.

Barbecued Crab Meat

Serves 6

¼ cup butter
½ teaspoon garlic powder
1 cup chopped onion
1½ cups chopped celery
1 can (10½ ounces) condensed chicken broth
1 soup can water
1 cup canned tomatoes
1 bay leaf
2 tablespoons Worcestershire sauce
½ teaspoon pepper
2 tablespoons soy sauce
1 teaspoon chopped parsley
1 tablespoon white vinegar
1 pound (about 2 cups) lump crab meat

Melt butter, add garlic powder; sauté onion and celery until tender but not brown. In a saucepan combine remaining ingredients except crab meat. Add onion-celery mixture. Cover and simmer for 1 hour or until sauce is thick. Remove bay leaf and fold in crab meat gently. Simmer 10 minutes. Spoon over rice or a nest of fine egg noodles. Serve with garlic bread.

Cream of Almond Soup

Serves 6

1 cup blanched almonds
2 tablespoons chopped onions
¼ cup chopped celery
1½ tablespoons butter
1½ tablespoons flour
1 can (10½ ounces) condensed cream of chicken soup
1 soup can water
1 cup light cream
¼ teaspoon white pepper
½ teaspoon salt
½ teaspoon almond extract

Toast almonds by heating them in a small skillet over medium heat. Stir occasionally. Grind almonds very fine. Sauté onions and celery in butter until golden. Stir in flour. Stir in cream of chicken soup, water, light cream, pepper, and salt. Add almonds. Simmer for 20 minutes, stirring occasionally. Stir in almond extract. Can be served hot or cold, topped with additional slivered, toasted almonds.

Wild Rice with Mushrooms

Serves 4 to 6

2 tablespoons chopped onion
⅓ cup butter
½ pound mushrooms, sliced
1 cup wild rice, washed
1 can (10½ ounces) condensed beef broth
¾ cup water
1 teaspoon salt

Sauté onion in butter until golden brown. Add mushrooms and sauté until wilted. Add remaining ingredients and pour mixture into 1-quart casserole. Cover and bake in a preheated 350°F. oven for 1 to 1½ hours. If desired, this dish may be cooked on top of the range. Leave in skillet, cover and simmer over low heat for 40 to 45 minutes, stirring occasionally.

Chicken Liver Casserole

Serves 4

8 chicken livers
⅓ cup butter
½ cup chopped onions
¼ cup sliced mushrooms
1 cup raw converted rice
2 teaspoons tomato catsup
1 can (10½ ounces) condensed chicken broth
1 cup water
¼ teaspoon black pepper
¼ teaspoon white pepper
½ cup grated sharp Cheddar cheese

Sauté chicken livers in butter. Remove livers from pan when just cooked and reserve. Add onions to pan drippings and sauté until wilted. Add mushrooms and sauté until soft. Add rice, catsup, and chicken broth, water, and black and white pepper. Pour mixture into a casserole, cover and bake in a preheated 350°F. oven for 40 minutes or until rice is tonder. Remove from oven and place chicken livers on top of rice. Sprinkle with cheese and bake for another 10 minutes or until cheese is melted.

Peanut Butter Soup

Serves 4 to 6

1 teaspoon minced onion
2 tablespoons butter
⅓ cup peanut butter
2 tablespoons flour
1 can (10½ ounces) condensed chicken broth
1¾ cups milk
½ cup heavy cream
Salt, pepper

Sauté onion in butter until pale brown. Remove from heat and add peanut butter and flour; stir until smooth. Gradually stir in chicken broth, milk, and cream. Cook over low heat, stirring constantly, until smooth and slightly thickened. Season to taste with salt and pepper.

Pontchartrain Wine Cellars

Detroit is not a quiet city. It does things on a bustling scale: brews beer, produces athletes, motorizes the world. But it also offers escape from the bustle in the Pontchartrain Wine Cellars, whose vast wine list and classic European food make it one of the great restaurants. The décor is as handsome and as satisfying as the food.

Bouillabaisse Marseillaise

Seafood Stew
Serves 6

¼ cup olive oil
1 can (1 pound, 12 ounces) tomatoes, chopped
½ cup chopped onion
3 cloves garlic, chopped
¼ teaspoon fennel seeds
½ teaspoon crushed thyme
1 bay leaf
2 tablespoons chopped parsley
½ teaspoon crushed rosemary
¼ cup minced celery
2 slices orange
2 slices lemon
1 cup dry white wine
2 cans (10½ ounces each) condensed chicken broth
¼ teaspoon crushed saffron
4 pounds assorted raw seafood—lobster, crab meat,
red snapper, cod, clams, whiting—cut into
bite-size pieces
Salt

In a Dutch oven or deep kettle heat olive oil. Add remaining ingredients except fish and salt. Bring to a boil, lower heat and simmer until vegetables are tender, about 15 minutes. Remove bay leaf, lemon and orange slices. If you are using lobster, drop into boiling water and cook only until shell turns red. Drain and drench with cold water. Cut the seafood—including lobster shell—into 1-inch pieces. Add fish pieces to soup. Simmer 10 minutes or until fish is cooked. Season to taste with salt. Serve bouillabaisse in soup bowls topped with toasted French bread slices or croutons and chopped parsley.

Dill Sauce

¼ cup butter
¼ cup flour
1 can (10½ ounces) condensed chicken broth
½ cup light cream
2 tablespoons chopped fresh dill or 1 tablespoon
dried dill weed
2 tablespoons white vinegar
2 teaspoons sugar
1 egg yolk, slightly beaten
Salt

Melt butter in a saucepan. Stir in flour. Gradually stir in chicken broth and cream. Cook, stirring, until sauce bubbles and thickens. Stir in dill, vinegar, and sugar. Beat some of the hot sauce into the egg yolk. Beat this into remaining sauce. Season to taste with salt. Reheat but do not boil. Spoon sauce over hot lamb shanks or sliced roast leg of lamb. Makes about 2 cups of sauce.

Left: Bouillabaisse Marseillaise

Adaptations from recipes by Chef Raymond D. Schwartz.

La Panetière

Often called "The Cradle of the Nation," Philadelphia is the city where the Declaration of Independence was written and signed, where the Constitution was molded, where the young nation was headquartered for many years. The Quakers, led by William Penn, first came to Philadelphia in 1681, and lived in caves along the Delaware River until houses could be built. Trade and commerce prospered under the industrious Quakers, and by Revolutionary times the city was a major center. There is much for the visitor to see: Independence Hall, Congress Hall, the Betsy Ross House, the United States Mint, the home where Edgar Allan Poe wrote "The Raven" and "The Gold Bug." A pleasant break in sight-seeing is a stop at La Panetière, a restaurant named after the French wall cupboard where bread is stored. Classic French cuisine is the order here, with many delightful *spécialités de la maison*.

Huîtres Pochées au Champagne

Oysters Poached in Champagne

Serves 4

36 large oysters
1 split bottle champagne
2 tablespoons white port
2 tablespoons dry vermouth
1 can (10 ounces) frozen condensed
oyster stew, thawed
¼ cup flour mixed with ¼ cup butter
2 egg yolks
½ cup grated Swiss cheese

Place shucked oysters in a saucepan. Add champagne, white port, and vermouth. Remove from heat as soon as the liquid begins to boil. Remove oysters with a slotted spoon and place in a shallow 1-quart casserole. Remove oysters from oyster stew and also place in casserole. Add liquid from oyster stew to champagne mixture. Drop flour-butter paste into hot liquid. Stir over low heat until sauce bubbles and thickens. Spoon sauce over oysters. Beat egg yolks and pour them evenly over the top of the casserole. Sprinkle top with grated cheese. Place the casserole under broiler and broil until top is bubbly and brown.

Rognon Braisé Dijonnaise

Braised Veal Kidneys

Serves 6

6 whole veal kidneys
¼ cup butter
¼ cup finely chopped shallots or white onions
4 crushed juniper berries
1 tablespoon white wine
1 tablespoon port wine
1 can (10½ ounces) condensed chicken broth
2 tablespoons cornstarch
¼ cup water
2 tablespoons Dijon mustard

Remove skin, fat, and muscle from kidneys and soak in cold water about half an hour. Heat butter and sauté kidneys until brown on all sides. Add shallots and juniper berries. Sauté until shallots are wilted. Add wines and chicken broth. Mix cornstarch with water and stir into sauce. Cook over low heat, stirring constantly, until sauce thickens. Stir in mustard.

Adapted by Chef Georges Perrier.

The Pavilion

When the magnificent Music Center opened in Los Angeles in 1964, so did one of the city's finest restaurants, The Pavilion, operated by Fred Harvey, Inc. Located on the top level of the Music Center, The Pavilion's dining room and cocktail lounge offer breathtaking panoramic views of the city. The aura is one of total elegance, the menu Continental. There are two beautiful banquet rooms—The Eldorado and The Blue Ribbon. Attending a private party in either can be a gastronomical event.

Veal Piccata Pavilion

Serves 6

12 veal scaloppini, pounded thin
2 small zucchini squash, cut into 1/4-inch slices
Salt, pepper
2 eggs, well beaten
1 cup flour
1/2 pound butter
1 tablespoon cornstarch
2 tablespoons sherry
1 can (10 1/2 ounces) condensed chicken broth
2 tablespoons lemon juice
2 tablespoons butter

Sprinkle veal and squash slices with salt and pepper. Dip veal and squash into eggs, then into flour. Melt part of the butter and sauté veal until golden brown, 5 to 6 minutes. Add squash and sauté on both sides, about 3 to 4 minutes. Add more butter as needed. Place veal on a platter; top each veal slice with 2 to 3 slices of zucchini. Keep warm. In a saucepan combine cornstarch and sherry. Gradually stir in chicken broth. Cook over low heat, stirring constantly, until sauce bubbles and thickens. Spoon sauce over veal. Sprinkle lemon juice over meat. Melt 2 tablespoons butter; cook until golden brown. Spoon brown butter over veal. Serve garnished with artichoke bottoms filled with tiny sweet peas.

Paella Valenciana

Serves 6 to 8

2 chickens, 2 to 2 1/2 pounds each, cut up
1/2 pound lean pork, cut into 3/4-inch cubes
1/4 pound lean veal, cut into 3/4-inch cubes
1/3 cup olive oil
1 clove garlic, minced
4 fresh tomatoes, chopped
3 cups raw converted rice
3 cans (10 1/2 ounces each) condensed chicken broth
2 cups water
1/2 teaspoon crumbled saffron
2 cans (8 ounces each) minced clams, undrained
1/2 pound raw shrimp, shelled and deveined
Salt, pepper

Sauté chicken, pork, and veal in olive oil in a large Dutch oven. When brown, add garlic, tomatoes; stir 1 minute. Add rice, broth, water, and saffron. Stir, lower heat. Cover; simmer, stirring occasionally, about 25 minutes or until rice is tender, liquid almost absorbed. Add clams, shrimp. Stir, cover; simmer another 10 minutes or until shrimp are cooked. Season to taste with salt and pepper.

Adapted from traditional recipes.

Putsch's 210

Because Kansas City, Missouri, is such a thoroughly American city, its Country Club Plaza is a particularly pleasant surprise. It is an area whose wide, tree-lined walks, eye-capturing sculpture, and classic urns and fountains create an aura of almost Mediterranean charm and a perfect setting for the Continental crystal-and-gold elegance of Putsch's 210 restaurant where the menu too is classic and Continental.

Breast of Capon Kiev

Serves 8

4 large capon or chicken breasts, halved, skinned, and boned
Salt, pepper, MSG
½ pound sweet butter
1 or 2 cloves garlic, chopped
1½ tablespoons chopped chives
1½ tablespoons chopped parsley
1 teaspoon salt
1 teaspoon crumbled rosemary
¼ teaspoon white pepper
1 can (10½ ounces) condensed cream of potato soup
¼ cup cream
2 tablespoons sherry
Flour
1 egg, well beaten
Deep fat or oil

Sprinkle each half breast with salt, pepper, and MSG. Pound capon between 2 pieces of wax paper until very thin but in one piece. Combine the butter, garlic, chives, parsley, salt, rosemary, and pepper. Mash until smooth. Divide mixture into 8 portions. Center one portion on each breast. Roll capon breasts around butter mixture to enclose butter completely. Chill. Combine soup, cream, and sherry. Whirl in a blender or press through a sieve. Heat until bubbly. Dip capon rolls into flour, then into beaten egg, and then again into flour. Fry in deep fat heated to 350°F. until golden brown. Place rolls in pan, uncovered; cook in pre-heated 350°F. oven for 30 to 35 minutes or until tender. To serve, arrange rolls on wild rice and spoon hot sauce over, so that each roll is liberally coated.

Turkey Madeira

Serves 4

2 tablespoons butter
1 can (10½ ounces) condensed chicken broth
12 thin slices cooked turkey breast
3 cups cooked wild rice
1 can (10¾ ounces) condensed vegetable beef soup
¼ cup Madeira wine

Heat butter and add chicken broth. When mixture is bubbling add turkey slices and simmer just until piping hot. Remove turkey slices and place on wild rice. (Reserve chicken broth and serve as a soup course.) Whirl vegetable beef soup and Madeira in a blender or press through a sieve. Heat mixture until bubbly. Spoon hot sauce over turkey and rice.

Left: Breast of Capon Kiev

Adaptations from recipes by Chef Herman Sanchez.

QVORVM

Called the "Mile High City," Denver, Colorado, began as a mining town, did not become a major city until the silver rush of the late nineteenth century. A delightful place to dine in Denver is the Quorum, which looks out over the gold-leafed dome of the Capitol and is elegantly Continental in décor and menu. Its owner and manager, Pierre Wolfe, a native of Alsace-Lorraine, received his chef's training in Switzerland. He supervises the preparation and service of all meals, and is also known to Denver television viewers as the host of the fascinating series, "Gourmet Cooking."

Frogs' Legs Provençale à la Quorum

Serves 4

8 pairs frogs' legs
Salt, pepper
Flour
⅓ cup oil
1 garlic clove, chopped
2 tablespoons minced onion
¼ cup dry white wine
1 teaspoon chopped parsley
1 teaspoon chopped chives
½ teaspoon dill seeds
1 tomato, peeled and chopped
1 can (11 ounces) condensed bisque of tomato soup

Soak frogs' legs in cold water 2 hours. Drain and pat dry. Sprinkle with salt and pepper. Dust with flour. In a skillet heat oil. Add garlic and onion; sauté until lightly browned. Add frogs' legs and sauté until pale brown. Add remaining ingredients and simmer until frogs' legs are tender, about 15 to 20 minutes. Serve over hot rice.

Left: Frogs' Legs Provençale à la Quorum

Lobster Newburg

Serves 4

4 frozen South African rock lobster tails,
4 ounces each
3 tablespoons butter
½ cup sherry
⅛ teaspoon paprika
⅛ teaspoon dry mustard
1 can (10½ ounces) condensed cream of
mushroom soup
⅓ cup light cream
Salt, pepper

Thaw lobster tails. With scissors cut through thin under membrane. Open out and remove meat in one piece. Dice meat and sauté in hot butter until it turns white and opaque. Add sherry. Simmer gently until the liquid is reduced to half its original volume and the lobster is tender. Add paprika, mustard, soup, and cream. Simmer 5 minutes. Season to taste with salt and pepper.

Adapted by Owner-Chef Pierre Wolfe.

Veal Slices Pyrénéenne

Serves 4

1 can (10½ ounces) condensed onion soup
2 tablespoons flour
2 egg yolks
½ cup light cream
2 tablespoons butter
8 veal scaloppini (Italian style or pounded very thin)
Flour
1 can (4 ounces) pâté de foie gras
16 mushroom caps
2 truffles, sliced
2 tablespoons chopped chives

Gradually stir onion soup into 2 tablespoons flour in a saucepan. Beat egg yolks with cream and stir into onion soup. Cook, stirring, over very low heat until sauce thickens. Do not boil. Keep sauce warm. Melt butter. Dip veal into flour and sauté in butter on both sides until brown. Place 4 of the slices of veal in a shallow casserole. Cut pâté into 4 slices and place slices on veal. Top with second 4 veal slices. Add mushroom caps, which have been sautéed in the pan drippings. Pour onion sauce over veal. Sprinkle with truffles, chives; place under broiler and broil until bubbly.

122   Pepper Steak with Onion Sauce

Serves 8

8 strip steaks
Freshly ground black pepper

Rub steaks with pepper and broil to desired degree of doneness. Sprinkle with salt after cooking. Serve with Onion Sauce.

Onion Sauce

1 can (10½ ounces) condensed onion soup
2 tablespoons butter
⅛ teaspoon dry mustard
½ cup tomato catsup
¼ to ½ cup A-1 sauce, according to taste
1 teaspoon Worcestershire sauce
Few drops liquid garlic
Finely chopped green onion tops

Combine onion soup, butter, mustard, catsup, A-1 sauce, Worcestershire sauce, and garlic in a saucepan. Simmer for 15 minutes. Spoon sauce over Pepper Steak or Scotch Eggs (see index). Sprinkle with green onion tops. Makes about 2½ cups of sauce.

Scotch Eggs

Serves 8

2 pounds ground round steak
1 clove garlic, minced
¼ teaspoon dry mustard
2 teaspoons salt
¼ teaspoon pepper
2 tablespoons grated onion
8 hard-cooked eggs
Flour
2 eggs, well beaten
1½ cups fine dry bread crumbs
Deep fat or oil for frying
Onion Sauce

Mix ground round, garlic, mustard, salt, pepper, and grated onion. Blend well and cut mixture into 8 pieces. Flatten each piece into a 4-inch round. Place 1 hard-cooked egg on each round. Shape meat around egg, enclosing it completely. Dip meat into flour, then into beaten egg, and then into bread crumbs. Chill for 1 hour. Fry in deep fat or oil, heated to 380°F., for 8 minutes or until brown on all sides. Cut each piece into halves crosswise. Place halves egg side up on a bed of crisp shoestring potatoes. Top with Onion Sauce.

Veal Belle Manière

Serves 4

8 slices veal, 3 ounces each
4 thin slices Mozzarella cheese
1 can (2¾ ounces) pâté de foie gras, chilled
Pepper
Flour
⅓ cup butter
1 can (10½ ounces) condensed cream of mushroom soup

Pound slices of veal until paper thin. Top 4 of the slices with a slice of cheese and a slice of the chilled pâté. Top with remaining veal slices and press together. Sprinkle both sides of the "sandwich" with pepper and dip into flour. Heat butter in a large skillet and brown veal on one side. Turn carefully and brown on the other side. Pour off excess fat. Spoon soup over veal, cover and simmer slowly for 10 minutes. Serve at once.

Stuffed Mushrooms Luxembourg

Serves 6

12 large fresh mushrooms
Boiling water
Juice of 1 lemon
3 tablespoons butter

Salt
1 shallot, minced
⅓ cup minced smoked tongue
1 cup dry white wine
1 can (8 ounces) pâté soufflé aux truffes
½ recipe Sauce Béchamel
¼ cup grated Parmesan cheese

Remove stems from mushrooms and wash caps and stems. Reserve stems. Place caps in a saucepan; add 1 cup boiling water, lemon juice, 1 tablespoon of the butter, and a dash of salt. Bring to a boil; boil for 3 to 5 minutes. Drain caps and place upside down in a shallow baking pan. Melt remaining butter and sauté shallot and tongue until shallot is wilted. Chop mushroom stems and add to pan. Sauté 5 minutes. Add white wine. Cook at a boil until wine is almost absorbed. Use mixture to stuff mushroom caps. Remove chilled pâté from can and cut into 12 thin slices. Place one slice over each filled mushroom. Spoon Sauce Béchamel over pâté. Sprinkle with grated cheese. Bake in a preheated 375°F. oven for 20 minutes or until top is lightly browned.

Parisian Turkey or Chicken
Serves 8

1 turkey, about 8 pounds (3 to 4 pounds of meat)
1 carrot, sliced
1 onion, sliced
1 bay leaf
6 peppercorns
1 tablespoon salt
1 can (10½ ounces) condensed cream of
mushroom soup
1 can (10½ ounces) condensed beef broth
¼ cup butter
1 egg yolk
1 tablespoon cornstarch
¼ cup water

In a large kettle place turkey, carrot, onion, bay leaf, peppercorns, and salt. Add water to cover turkey. Cover and simmer until turkey is tender, about 2 hours. Drain and reserve broth for future use in soups and gravies. Cool turkey; then skin and bone. Dice meat into cubes. In a saucepan combine mushroom soup, beef broth, and butter. Beat egg yolk, cornstarch, and water until smooth. Stir this mixture into soups gradually. Heat, stirring, until sauce bubbles and thickens. Fold in turkey. Spoon over rice.

Brown Rice
Serves 4

¼ cup minced onion
¼ cup butter
1 cup raw converted rice
1 can (10½ ounces) condensed consommé
1 cup water
Salt

Sauté onion in butter in a large saucepan. Add rice and sauté until rice is golden. Add consommé and water. Cover and simmer until rice is tender, stirring occasionally, until rice has absorbed all the liquid, about 20 to 25 minutes. Season to taste with salt.

Sauce Béchamel

123

¼ cup minced onions
¼ cup butter
1 can (10½ ounces) condensed cream of
chicken soup
2 egg yolks
¾ cup heavy cream

Sauté onions in butter until pale golden brown. Stir soup, egg yolks, and cream into onions. Cook over low heat, stirring constantly, until sauce bubbles and thickens. Sauce Béchamel is a basic sauce. It can be pressed through a strainer if a smooth sauce is desired. Makes about 2 cups of sauce.

TOLL GATE LODGE

These days there's no romance involved in paying a traveler's toll. One tosses one's coin into the impersonal basket on the throughway and drives on. But in the days of the stagecoach, a tollgate was often an excuse for a stop at a nearby inn, where the driver acquired fresh horses and the passengers refreshed themselves with food, drink, and gossip. Modern-day travelers can still refresh themselves—and very well too—at the Toll Gate Lodge in Manchester, Vermont, which marks a favorite stopping place of the old Boston-to-Saratoga Springs coach. The lovely setting remains as it was a hundred and more years ago, but the horses are long since gone and perhaps the local gossip wouldn't mean much to those just passing through. The Toll Gate's fine French food, however, is far more elegant fare than ever fell to the lot of those long-ago travelers. The Lodge is owned by Barbara and Mario Berry.

Cremolata Sauce

2 tablespoons butter
1 pound salt pork, finely diced
4 stalks celery, finely diced
4 small onions, finely diced
4 medium carrots, finely diced
1 cup dry white wine
2 cans (10½ ounces each) condensed consommé
Grated rind of 1 large lemon
2 tablespoons finely chopped garlic
¼ cup finely chopped parsley

Combine butter, salt pork, celery, onions, and carrots in a saucepan. Sauté until vegetables are tender. Add white wine and cook at a boil until wine is almost absorbed. Add consommé and simmer for 15 minutes. Strain mixture. Discard salt pork and vegetables. Add lemon rind, garlic, and parsley to strained liquid. Simmer for 1 minute, then spoon over filet or veal. Can be refrigerated for future use. Makes 2 cups.

Adapted by Owner-Chef Mario Berry.

Sea Bass en Papillote Maison
Serves 4

4 small fillets of sea bass
Salt, pepper
¼ cup butter
8 shrimp, peeled and deveined
8 thin slices lemon
2 tablespoons crumbled bleu cheese
1 can (10½ ounces) condensed cream of mushroom soup

Sprinkle fish on both sides with salt and pepper. Place butter in the center of each of 4 pieces of aluminum foil 3 times the size of the piece of fish. Place fish over butter. Top each piece of fish with 2 shrimp and 2 slices lemon. Combine bleu cheese and soup. Spoon mixture over fish. Fold foil over twice loosely and then turn up ends so sauce will not leak out. Bake in a preheated 350°F. oven for 25 to 30 minutes or until fish flakes.

Perdita's

The 180-year-old brick building that houses Perdita's in Charleston, South Carolina, has been a landmark on cobblestoned Exchange Street since Revolutionary days. In the main dining room hangs a copy of Gainsborough's portrait of Mrs. Paul Robinson, the Shakespearean actress famous for her portrayal of Perdita in "A Winter's Tale." Both the atmosphere and the food of today's Perdita's are delightful.

Baked Shrimp and Lobster en Papillote

Serves 6

1½ tablespoons French-style prepared mustard
¼ cup sour cream
1½ teaspoons chopped chives
¼ cup Chablis or other dry white wine
3 cups cooked medium shrimp, fresh or
frozen, shelled and deveined
3 cups diced cooked fresh lobster pieces or *cooked*
frozen South African rock lobster tails
6 pieces heavy duty aluminum foil, cut in
12-inch squares
6 tablespoons butter
1 large lemon, cut into 12 slices
1 can (10¾ ounces) condensed Cheddar cheese soup
Nutmeg, salt, pepper

In a saucepan combine mustard, sour cream, chives, and wine. Stir to blend; heat just to the boiling point. Remove from heat; cool. Combine shrimp and lobster; place 1 cup on each square of foil. Top each with 1 tablespoon of the butter, 2 lemon slices, 3⅓ tablespoons of Cheddar cheese soup, 1½ tablespoons of wine-mustard sauce. Sprinkle with nutmeg, salt, and pepper. Fold together 2 edges of the foil in a drugstore fold. Seal ends tightly. Place packets on cookie sheet. Bake in a preheated 450°F. oven 10 to 15 minutes or until packets are puffed. Serve in foil by slitting each side of the center fold; pull up center fold to shape a handle, push back sides to shape a basket. *Note:* These packets can be prepared ahead, refrigerated until ready to cook. Allow 5 extra minutes' baking time.

She Crab and Shrimp Soup

Serves 6

¼ cup butter
1 small onion, finely chopped
¾ cup white crab meat
1 ounce crab roe (if available)
¾ cup cooked small shrimp
½ cup flour
1 teaspoon paprika
Dash MSG
1 can (10 ounces) frozen condensed cream of shrimp
soup, thawed
1 quart milk
2 tablespoons sherry
Salt, pepper

In a saucepan melt butter; sauté onion until tender but not brown. Add crab meat, roe, shrimp, flour, paprika, MSG. Add shrimp soup; gradually stir in milk. Add sherry. Stir over low heat until soup thickens slightly, just starts to bubble. Season to taste. Add a little sherry to each serving at the table.

Adapted by Owner Gordon W. Bennett.

River Ranch

In the Sierra Nevadas near the Carson Pass, in a part of California dedicated to the outdoor life, lies Lake Tahoe—and the River Ranch. This handsome wood-and-stone lodge was designed for active sports fans: in winter, it houses skiers and skaters, in summer fishermen, tennis and riding buffs, and even those who take their exercise simply walking along the awesomely beautiful trails. Sturdy fare for appetites sharpened by hours of fresh air is not always elegant. But the River Ranch kitchen gives the lie to that idea with an intriguing style of its own, providing a menu rich in hearty dishes of gourmet stature and the appropriate domestic and imported wines.

Lobster Pompadour

Serves 6

1 can (2 ounces) sliced mushrooms
1 cup sliced celery
½ teaspoon chervil, crushed
¼ cup butter or margarine
2 cans (10 ounces each) frozen condensed cream of shrimp soup, thawed
1 can (10¾ ounces) condensed tomato soup
1 cup light cream
3 cups cubed cooked lobster
6 frozen patty shells, baked

In a saucepan, brown mushrooms and cook celery with chervil in butter until tender. Add soups, cream, and lobster. Heat, stirring occasionally. Serve Lobster Pompadour in patty shells.

Breast of Chicken Chantilly

Serves 4

2 breasts of chicken, cut in half

Left: Lobster Pompadour

¼ cup butter
1 package (9 ounces) frozen artichoke hearts, cooked and drained
1 package (10 ounces) frozen asparagus spears, cooked and drained
1 can (10½ ounces) condensed chicken broth
1 can (10½ ounces) condensed cream of mushroom soup
½ cup heavy cream, whipped

In a skillet, brown chicken breasts in butter slowly for about 30 minutes or until chicken is well cooked and tender. Remove chicken breasts to a platter and surround with hot vegetables. Keep warm. Add chicken broth and cream of mushroom soup to the pan drippings. Simmer until sauce is thick, about 15 minutes. Fold in cream; pour sauce over chicken and vegetables. Serve at once. *Note:* This sauce should be prepared as close to the last minute as possible. If it is kept hot for too long it will become thin.

Adapted by Maître d' Franz Fassbender.

Rod's Shadowbrook

A more pleasant place than a small town in the central part of New Jersey, close to the beautiful Jersey shore, would be hard to imagine. Here, in the pretty town of Shrewsbury, is Rod's Shadowbrook, operated by Rod Keller, one of the three delightful dining places under the sponsorship of members of the Keller family in New Jersey. For his Shadowbrook, Rod Keller decided on the Victorian era—all rococo opulence—as the theme around which to center the decoration. The main dining room is wood-paneled, and the tables are set with china, silver, and glassware reminiscent of Victorian days. The walls are graced by paintings of that bygone era, and the menu, with its Continental entrées, carries out the romantic elegance of a time long past.

Gazpacho

Cold Tomato-Vegetable Soup

Serves 6 to 7

1 clove garlic, chopped
1 cucumber, peeled, seeded, and chopped
1 small green pepper, seeded and chopped
½ onion, chopped
2 ripe tomatoes, peeled, seeded, and chopped
2 cans (10¾ ounces each) condensed tomato soup
2 soup cans water
2 tablespoons olive oil
¼ cup lemon juice
1 teaspoon salt
Dash Tabasco sauce

Rub soup tureen with chopped garlic, then discard garlic. Put cucumber, green pepper, onion, and tomatoes in tureen. Mix tomato soup and water, and add to tureen with remaining ingredients. Chill until icy cold and serve sprinkled with tiny crisp croutons. Serve in bowls with an ice cube in each bowl. *Note:* Gazpacho can be the main course of a light meal.

Left: Gazpacho

Sliced Filet Mignon Zingara

Serves 4

8 slices filet mignon, 3 ounces each
1 tablespoon oil
½ to 1 cup Burgundy wine, according to taste
1 shallot, minced, or 1 tablespoon minced green onions
¼ teaspoon crumbled thyme
½ bay leaf
1 can (10½ ounces) condensed golden mushroom soup
½ cup julienne strips boiled ham

Brown filets in oil on both sides and put on hot serving dish. Keep warm. Slices should be rare. To pan drippings, add Burgundy, shallot, thyme, and bay leaf. Boil until liquid is reduced to half its original volume. Remove bay leaf. Stir in mushroom soup. Simmer until thick and bubbly. Add ham strips and spoon sauce over filets. Sprinkle with chopped parsley and serve at once.

Adapted by Chef Hans Pfeiffer.

Poor Richard's Tavern

Down Easters are accustomed to austerity. They take their cue from the bared-to-the-bone beauty of Maine's rockbound shores, and make a virtue of plain, undecorated living. But plain is one thing, and deprived is another. The day Poor Richard's Tavern opened in Perkin's Cove, Ogunquit, the two young proprietors found themselves living somewhat more "plain" than they had bargained for—with mismatched china, rickety furniture, and fifteen cents making a most unsatisfying rattle in the till. Things happily have changed since then for "Poor Richard" Perkins and Robert Maurais. Nowadays, Maine natives, travelers, and the many part-time residents who have made Perkin's Cove a burgeoning art colony know the Tavern as an enclave bathed in candlelit luxury, where the atmosphere is on the formal side. A suitably respectful approach to such dishes as Chicken Divan, Boeuf Bourguignon, and the many other delicacies on the menu have established the Tavern's varied cuisine as among the most outstanding to be found in the New England states.

Boeuf Bourguignon
Beef in Burgundy Sauce
Serves 6

3 pounds lean beef chuck, cut into 1-inch cubes
1 can (10½ ounces) condensed consommé
1 cup "V-8" juice
1 cup Burgundy wine
½ cup firmly packed brown sugar
1 can (10½ ounces) condensed onion soup
½ teaspoon garlic powder
1 teaspoon oregano
½ teaspoon celery salt
2 bay leaves
3 tablespoons cornstarch
⅓ cup water

Combine all ingredients except cornstarch and water in a large saucepan. Cover and simmer slowly until meat is tender, about 2 hours. Stir occasionally. Remove bay leaves. Combine cornstarch and water and stir mixture into hot stew. Cook until sauce thickens.

Chicken Divan
Serves 4

1 can (10¾ ounces) condensed
Cheddar cheese soup
¼ cup brandy
½ teaspoon garlic powder
¼ teaspoon celery salt
¼ teaspoon crumbled basil
1 package (10 ounces) frozen broccoli spears
2 whole chicken breasts, cooked, skinned, and sliced

Combine soup, brandy, garlic powder, celery salt, and basil. Heat until bubbly. Cook broccoli spears until tender but still firm. Place broccoli in a shallow baking pan; top with chicken slices. Spoon sauce over all. Bake in a preheated 375°F. oven for 20 minutes or until mixture is bubbly.

Adapted by Owner Richard W. Perkins.

Primos

Named for Andrew Jackson, and designed in a checkerboard pattern at the suggestion of Thomas Jefferson, the city of Jackson, Mississippi, still retains evidence of the planners' design. Every other square was reserved for a park or a green. During the Civil War, the city was besieged and burned by General Sherman. Sub Rosa Plantation Home, open to the public, is one of the few buildings not destroyed at that time. The State Capitol is a replica of the nation's Capitol in Washington and the governor's mansion resembles the White House—both are worth seeing. Another must in present-day Jackson is a visit to Primos Northgate, a building complex that includes ten private dining rooms, the Country Kitchen, the Golden Horse, the Sea Food Bar, a delicatessen, and a bakery. Each of the restaurants offers an appropriate menu of the regional and traditional specialties for which Primos Northgate is famous.

Tomato Soup Salad

Serves 6 to 8

3 envelopes unflavored gelatin
2½ cups water
2 cans (10¾ ounces each) condensed tomato soup
1 package (8 ounces) cream cheese
2 tablespoons light cream
½ cup sliced stuffed olives

Soak gelatin in ¾ cup of the water 5 minutes. Stir over low heat until gelatin is dissolved. Stir gelatin and remaining water gradually into tomato soup. Pour half of the mixture into a lightly oiled 9- x 9-inch pan. Chill until firm. Mash cream cheese until soft. Beat in cream. Fold in olives. Spread mixture evenly and carefully over firm gelatin. Pour remaining tomato mixture over cheese. Chill until firm. Cut into serving-size pieces, using a sharp knife. Loosen edges and remove pieces with a pancake turner. Serve salad on lettuce leaves with mayonnaise, garnished with finely chopped parsley.

Soupy Chicken

Serves 6

1 can (10½ ounces) condensed cream of
mushroom soup
1 can (10½ ounces) condensed cream of chicken soup
1 can (10½ ounces) condensed cream of celery soup
½ cup light cream
¼ cup melted butter
1½ cups raw rice
1 frying chicken, about 3 pounds, cut up
Salt, pepper, paprika
¼ cup butter

Combine soups, cream, melted butter, and rice. Spread mixture into a lightly greased 9- x 12- x 2-inch baking pan. Top with chicken pieces. Sprinkle chicken with salt, pepper, and paprika. Dot top with butter. Bake in a preheated 350°F. oven for 1½ hours, or until the chicken and rice are tender. Serve Soupy Chicken garnished with parsley.

Adapted by Martha H. Lyell.

SEÑOR PICO

Mexico, Spain, and early California blend at Señor Pico's, in Century City, to evoke the California of another day. From south-of-the-border antiques to the regional specialties on its unusual menu, this romantic restaurant creates a scene in which an early settler would have been quite at home. There is also a Señor Pico's (complete with attractive gift shop) in San Francisco's famed Ghirardelli Square.

Cheese Enchiladas
Serves 6

¼ cup chopped onion
1 tablespoon butter or *margarine*
2 cups cottage cheese
1 pound white Cheddar cheese, shredded
¼ cup crushed tostadas
2 tablespoons chopped stuffed olives
2 tablespoons chopped jalapeño chilies
1 teaspoon salt
1 teaspoon MSG
12 tortillas
Green Enchilada Sauce

Cook onion in butter until tender. Add cheeses, tostadas, olives, chilies, and seasonings. Fry tortillas in oil until soft and pliable but not crisp. Drain; center cheese filling in each tortilla and roll. Place in greased shallow baking dish, seam side down. Add Green Enchilada Sauce.

Green Enchilada Sauce

1 can (10½ ounces) condensed chicken broth
1 cup snipped spinach leaves
2 cans (10½ ounces) condensed cream of mushroom soup
1 can (3½ ounces) Ortega chilies
1 large onion, diced
1 clove garlic, sliced

Left: Cheese Enchiladas with Green Enchilada Sauce

1 teaspoon MSG
½ teaspoon salt
2 tablespoons flour
½ pint sour cream

Combine chicken broth and spinach in blender. Blend until smooth. Pour into saucepan. Blend cream of mushroom soup, chilies, onion, and garlic until smooth; add to spinach mixture. Stir in MSG and salt. Simmer 10 to 15 minutes. Thicken sauce with flour mixed with a little water. Pour over Cheese Enchiladas. Bake in a preheated 350°F. oven for 20 minutes. Top with sour cream before serving.

Texas Chili
Serves 6

1 large onion, chopped
1 clove garlic, minced
3 tablespoons oil
1 pound ground round steak
½ teaspoon cumin seed
2 cans (11 ounces each) condensed chili beef soup
1¼ cups water

Sauté onion and garlic in oil until golden. Add ground round and sauté until meat is brown and crumbly. Drain off excess fat; stir in remaining ingredients. Cover and simmer, stirring occasionally, until thickened, about 20 minutes. Add salt to taste, if desired.

Adapted by Owner Trader Vic.

Baked Lamb Chops

Serves 8

8 double loin chops, trimmed
Salt, pepper
⅓ cup flour
¼ cup butter
½ pound fresh mushrooms, sliced
1 clove garlic, minced
1 cup sliced celery
¼ cup chopped parsley
¼ teaspoon crumbled oregano
1 can (10½ ounces) condensed onion soup
½ cup white wine
8 small carrots, sliced, cooked, and drained
1 can (1 pound) onions, drained
1 can (8 ounces) pitted black olives, drained
1 package (10 ounces) frozen peas
2 teaspoons lemon juice

Sprinkle chops with salt and pepper. Dip into flour and coat completely. Brown chops on both sides in butter. Place chops in a shallow casserole side by side. To pan drippings, add mushrooms, garlic, celery, and parsley. Sauté until vegetables are wilted. Add oregano, onion soup, and wine. Pour mixture over lamb chops. Cover and bake in a preheated 350°F. oven for 30 minutes. Stir in carrots, onions, black olives, and peas. Cover and bake another 30 minutes. Remove from oven and stir in lemon juice. Season to taste with salt and pepper. Serve with steamed rice, buttered noodles, or mashed potatoes.

134

Chilies Rellenos con Queso

Peppers Stuffed with Cheese
Serves 6

6 canned green chilies
6 pieces Monterey Jack cheese, ½ x ½ x 2 inches
6 pieces sharp Cheddar cheese, ½ x ½ x 2 inches
Flour
6 egg whites
6 egg yolks
¼ cup melted butter, cooled

Sauce

½ cup chopped onions
1 clove garlic, minced
1 tablespoon oil
2 tablespoons chili sauce
1 cup chopped canned tomatoes
1 tablespoon flour

1 can (10½ ounces) condensed beef broth
1 teaspoon sugar
½ teaspoon salt
1 teaspoon white vinegar

Drain chilies and stuff each with 1 piece of each kind of cheese. Roll stuffed chilies in flour. Butter 6 small individual casseroles. Beat egg whites until stiff. Beat egg yolks until thick and lemon-colored. Fold egg yolks and cooled butter into egg whites. Divide half of the egg mixture among the casseroles. Top with stuffed chilies. Spoon remaining egg mixture over chilies. Bake in a preheated 350°F. oven for 25 minutes. *To prepare sauce,* sauté onions and garlic in oil until golden. Blend in chili sauce, tomatoes, and flour. Stir in beef broth, sugar, salt, and vinegar. Cook over medium heat, stirring, until sauce bubbles and thickens. Spoon sauce over baked chilies.

Albondiga Soup

Serves 6 to 8

Soup

½ cup finely chopped onion
1 clove garlic, chopped
2 tablespoons oil
1 teaspoon chili powder
1 can (11 ounces) condensed bisque of
tomato soup
3 cans (10½ ounces each) condensed consommé
3 soup cans water

Meatballs

½ pound ground beef
½ pound ground pork
½ cup cooked rice
1 tablespoon cornstarch
⅛ teaspoon garlic powder
¼ teaspoon oregano
1 teaspoon salt
¼ teaspoon pepper
1 egg
¼ cup chopped parsley

Sauté onion and garlic in oil until limp but not brown. Add chili powder, soups, and water. Simmer for 20 minutes. While soup is simmering, combine remaining ingredients except parsley, mix well and shape into balls about the size of a walnut. Drop balls into simmering soup. Simmer for an additional 30 minutes. To serve, pour into Mexican pottery bowl and ladle out into individual pottery bowls, putting several meatballs in each bowl and sprinkling with a little chopped parsley.

Rabbit, Mexican Style

Serves 6

2 rabbits, about 1 or 1½ pounds each
½ cup peanut oil
2 small chili peppers
2 cloves garlic, crushed
Flour
2 tablespoons butter
1 large carrot, finely diced
½ cup finely chopped onion
3 tablespoons finely chopped green pepper
1 cup chopped mushrooms
1 tablespoon flour
1 can (10½ ounces) condensed chicken broth
Juice of 1 small orange
2 tablespoons finely shredded orange peel
2 tablespoons peanut butter
½ teaspoon cumin seeds
1 tablespoon toasted sesame seeds
3 whole cloves
Dash nutmeg
Salt, pepper
1 tablespoon chopped parsley

Cut legs from rabbits and cut backs in three pieces. In a Dutch oven heat oil and add chili peppers. Fry peppers until brown, crushing them to extract juice. Remove peppers. Rub pieces of rabbit with garlic and then coat with flour. Brown pieces of rabbit in the oil until golden brown on all sides. Cover and simmer until rabbit is tender, about 1 to 1½ hours. Pour off excess fat. *To prepare sauce,* melt butter in a large saucepan. Sauté carrot, onion, green pepper, and mushrooms. When vegetables are soft, stir in flour. Gradually stir in chicken broth and orange juice. Cook over low heat, stirring constantly, until sauce bubbles and thickens slightly. Add orange peel, peanut butter, cumin seeds, sesame seeds, cloves, nutmeg, and salt and pepper to taste. Simmer sauce about 15 minutes, stirring occasionally. Place rabbit on a platter. Skim excess fat from top of sauce and spoon sauce over rabbit pieces. Sprinkle with chopped parsley.

Chicken Tacos

Makes 12 tacos

1 large onion, finely chopped
2 tablespoons oil
2 cups coarsely chopped cooked chicken
1 cup Red Enchilada Sauce
½ teaspoon salt
12 tortillas
Cooking oil

Sauté onions in oil until limp; stir in chicken, Enchilada Sauce, and salt. Simmer until mixture is thick. To prepare tortillas, fry in hot oil about 1 inch deep until soft and pliable. Fold tortilla in half in pan, using a spatula. Hold in place until tortilla is crisp. Turn and fry other side. Drain on absorbent paper. Open carefully and fill with chicken mixture.

Red Enchilada Sauce

¼ cup finely chopped onions
½ teaspoon minced garlic
2 tablespoons oil
1 can (10½ ounces) condensed chicken broth
1 soup can water
1½ tablespoons chili powder
¼ cup flour
1½ teaspoons MSG
1 tablespoon oil
½ cup chili sauce

Sauté onions and garlic in oil until transparent. Add broth and water. Combine remaining ingredients and mix into paste. Stir paste into broth. Stir and simmer for 15 minutes. Makes 2½ cups of sauce.

Baked Green Beans

Serves 4

1 pound green beans
3 slices bacon, diced
1 large onion, chopped
1 cup sliced mushrooms
1 can (10½ ounces) condensed chicken broth
¼ teaspoon pepper
½ teaspoon MSG

Remove ends of green beans and wash and drain. Arrange beans in a shallow casserole. In skillet fry bacon until crisp. Add onions, mushrooms; sauté until wilted but not brown. Stir in remaining ingredients. Pour over green beans. Cover and bake in a preheated 350°F. oven for 40 to 45 minutes or until beans are easily pierced. Remove from oven. If desired, liquid in casserole may be thickened with 2 teaspoons cornstarch mixed with 2 tablespoons water. Cook until broth is thickened.

Russian Tea Room

At Carnegie Hall, in New York City, all the greats of the soloist and orchestra worlds have appeared to charm audiences for more than a century. Next door to Carnegie the Russian Tea Room is ideally located as a meeting place for theater and music personalities. At almost any time the visitor will be able to see a famous conductor at his favorite table, or a ballerina—perhaps in practice clothes—having a snack before returning to rehearsal, or a well-known critic enjoying a late supper while considering what he will say in tomorrow's review. The food is delicious, the atmosphere simple and informal—but, to the celebrity-hunter, heady. Lunch, dinner, and after-theater supper are served, offering authentic Russian cuisine. Among the many memorable specialties of the Russian Tea Room are its Borschts and Stroganoffs.

Hot Borscht with Vegetables
Serves 6 to 8

1 bunch beets (4 or 5 beets about 2 inches in diameter), peeled and grated
2 cans (10½ ounces each) condensed beef broth
2 cans (10½ ounces each) condensed onion soup
3 cups finely shredded green cabbage
4 cups water
2 cans (10¾ ounces each) condensed old-fashioned vegetable soup
1 teaspoon salt
2 tablespoons sugar
2 tablespoons MSG
2 tablespoons finely chopped fresh dill or 1 tablespoon dried dill weed

Combine grated beets, beef broth, onion soup, green cabbage, and water. Cook covered over medium heat until beets and cabbage are tender. Stir in remaining ingredients and simmer another 10 minutes. Serve hot, topped with sour cream and additional chopped fresh dill, if desired.

Mushrooms à la Russe
Serves 6

2 pounds mushrooms
Juice of ½ lemon
2 cans (10½ ounces each) condensed cream of mushroom soup
1 tablespoon butter
⅓ cup heavy cream
⅓ cup sour cream
Salt, pepper

Wash mushrooms, drain and slice. Cover with water, add lemon juice, and simmer until mushrooms are tender, about 10 minutes. Drain. Combine soup, butter, heavy cream, and sour cream. Heat until bubbly. Fold in sliced mushrooms. Reheat and season to taste with salt and pepper. Serve spooned over toast or split hot biscuits. These delicious mushrooms in sauce may be used as a filling for crêpes, if desired.

Adaptations from recipes by Chef George Lohen.

The Simon House

The story of The Simon House, in Madison, Wisconsin, goes back to 1833, when a German named John Simon felt that his fellow immigrants needed a place in which to savor the familiar dishes of the old country in a setting that reminded them of home. The Simon House has gone through several radical changes since John Simon's time, yet somehow the relaxed and welcoming atmosphere that he created still prevails. Nowadays it serves fine, imaginative food in a softly lit, richly draped room in which the diner is likely to feel like a charter member of a luxuriously comfortable and very friendly club where he is made welcome—and where he is certain to be fed superbly.

Simon House au Gratin

Serves 6

6 slices toast
12 thin slices smoked cooked ham
2 cans (10½ ounces each) golden mushroom soup
½ cup heavy cream
2 cups (8 ounces) grated sharp Cheddar cheese

Place toast in a shallow baking dish. Top with ham slices. Combine soup and cream and spoon over ham. Sprinkle top with grated cheese. Bake in a preheated 400°F. oven for 15 to 20 minutes or until cheese is melted and lightly browned.

Tenderloin Tips à la Rossoni

Serves 6

6 tenderloin slices, cut 1 inch thick
6 slices calves' liver
Salt, pepper
6 large mushroom caps
¼ cup butter
1 can (10½ ounces) condensed cream of
mushroom soup
⅓ cup light cream

Sprinkle meat and liver on both sides with salt and pepper. Sauté meat, liver, and mushrooms in butter until golden brown and cooked to the desired degree of doneness. Remove meat from pan. Pour mushroom soup and cream in the pan and stir until all the brown bits on the bottom of the pan are mixed in; heat until sauce just begins to bubble. Serve sauce over meat.

Chicken Maurice

Serves 6

3 whole chicken breasts, cooked, skinned, and boned
2 cans (10½ ounces each) condensed cream of
chicken soup
1 can (15½ ounces) boiled onions, drained
½ cup juice drained from onions
1 can (1 pound) baby whole carrots, drained
1 can (4 ounces) chopped mushrooms, drained
⅓ cup slivered almonds

Cut cooked chicken into slices. Put slices in a skillet. Add soup, boiled onions, onion juice, carrots, and mushrooms. Heat just until bubbly and hot. Sprinkle with slivered almonds.

Adapted by Chef Maurice Coombs.

The Spanish Pavilion

A contract from his government to direct the Marisqueria and Bar Barcelona at the New York World's Fair brought Alberto Heras to the United States in 1964. With the Fair's closing, Señor Heras and his wife decided to establish a permanent base in this country. They opened The Spanish Pavilion, on New York's fabled Park Avenue, to serve *alta cocina Española*—first-class Spanish food—which is prepared by few, if any, restaurants in this country. The Spanish Pavilion is handsome in classic Spanish style—a rendezvous for discriminating and sophisticated diners.

Zarzuela de Mariscos "Costa Brava"

Spanish Seafood Stew

Serves 6 to 8

1 lobster, about 1½ pounds, cooked just until red
1 carrot, minced
1 leek, minced
2 celery stalks, minced
1 small onion, chopped
6 tablespoons butter
1 teaspoon paprika
1 cup white wine
1 cup cognac
1 can (10½ ounces) condensed chicken
with rice soup
1 can (10½ ounces) beef broth
1 pound tomatoes, chopped
⅛ teaspoon almond extract
12 jumbo shrimp, raw, shelled, and deveined
12 red Spanish shrimp, raw, shelled, and deveined
12 littleneck clams, scrubbed
12 mussels, beards removed, scrubbed
1 red snapper fillet, about ½ pound, cut into
1-inch cubes

⅓ cup olive oil
Salt, pepper

Remove head from lobster and grind or pound in a mortar until particles are very fine. Cut remaining lobster into slices. In a kettle combine lobster head, carrot, leek, celery, onion, and butter. Sauté until onion is golden. Add paprika, wine, and cognac. Set aflame. When flame dies, add chicken soup, beef broth, tomatoes, and almond extract. Simmer gently, stirring occasionally, until mixture is very thick, about 2 hours. Pour into a strainer and press out all liquid for sauce. In a large skillet combine lobster slices, jumbo shrimp, Spanish shrimp, clams, mussels, red snapper, and olive oil. Sauté until fish is cooked and clams and mussels are open, about 10 minutes. Drain excess liquid and reserve ½ cup of this broth. Add lobster sauce and reserved broth (about 1½ cups of total liquid). Simmer for 10 minutes uncovered. Add salt and pepper to taste. When serving, place a variety of seafood on individual plates, top with some of the sauce. Garnish each serving with chopped parsley and tarragon, and with quartered slices of white bread fried in olive oil.

Left: Zarzuela de Mariscos "Costa Brava"

Adaptations from recipes by Chef Mariano Bocos.

Sopa Cuarto de Hora
Quarter Hour Soup
Serves 6 to 8

4 tablespoons olive oil
1 clove garlic, chopped
½ pound fresh shrimp, shelled, deveined, diced
1 can (10½ ounces) condensed onion soup
1 can (11 ounces) condensed bisque of tomato soup
2 soup cans water
⅛ teaspoon crumbled saffron
1 tablespoon minced parsley
½ pound chicken livers
¼ cup raw rice, cooked and drained
1 hard-cooked egg, finely chopped

Heat 2 tablespoons olive oil and sauté garlic until golden. Add shrimp and continue cooking until shrimp become pink and opaque. Add soups, water, saffron and parsley. Stir and simmer for 5 minutes. Heat 2 tablespoons olive oil and sauté chicken livers until brown and well cooked, about 10 minutes. Cube livers; add livers, cooked rice, and egg to soup. Simmer 5 minutes. Serve with cubed white bread sautéed in olive oil until golden brown.

Pisto Manchego
Vegetable Stew
Serves 6

1 can (10½ ounces) condensed onion soup
2 leeks, chopped
4 canned red pimientos, cut into strips
3 green peppers, seeded and diced
2 yellow squash, cubed
2 large fresh tomatoes, chopped
2 slices boiled or smoked ham,
4 x 6 inches, cubed
2 tablespoons butter
2 tablespoons oil
4 eggs, well beaten
Salt

Combine soup, leeks, pimientos, peppers, squash, tomatoes, ham, butter, and oil. Bring to a boil, lower heat and simmer for 30 to 35 minutes, or until mixture is thick and liquid is almost absorbed. Stir in beaten eggs, cook 2 to 3 minutes longer. (Should be con-

sistency of thick stew.) Season to taste with salt. Serve the Pisto very hot.

Sopa Castilla la Vieja
Almond Soup
Serves 6

3 cans (10½ ounces each) condensed consommé
3 soup cans water
½ cup ground blanched almonds
1 tablespoon olive oil
3 slices bread, toasted, cut into 1-inch strips
⅓ cup grated Parmesan cheese
½ cup toasted sliced almonds

Heat consommé and water. Mix almonds and oil and add to soup. Beat until well blended. Spoon soup into individual heat-proof bowls. Top bowls with toast strips. Sprinkle with cheese. Broil until cheese is golden. Sprinkle with sliced almonds.

Lenguado Spanish Pavilion
Fillet of Sole, Spanish Pavilion Style
Serves 4

4 fillets of sole, cut into 1-inch strips
10 red Spanish shrimp (or regular large or extra-large shrimp)
1 shallot, minced, or 1 tablespoon minced green onion
1½ cups sherry
2 pimientos, diced
¼ pound fresh mushrooms, sliced
6 large pitted green olives, sliced
2 tablespoons butter
1 can (10½ ounces) condensed cream of chicken soup
1 egg yolk
¼ cup heavy cream
1 teaspoon lemon juice

Combine sole, shelled and deveined shrimp (reserve two for sauce; mince these two shrimp), shallot, and sherry. Cook gently until sole and shrimp are just cooked. With a slotted spoon remove sole and shrimp and arrange in a 9-inch-square shallow baking pan. Add minced shrimp to sherry mixture and simmer until liquid is reduced to ½ cup. Reserve. Sauté pimientos, mushrooms, and olives in butter until mushrooms are wilted. Spoon vegetables over sole and shrimp. Combine soup, egg yolk, reserved sherry, and cream. Heat slowly, stirring constantly until hot, but do not boil. Remove from heat and stir in lemon juice. Spoon sauce evenly over sole and shrimp. Place under broiler and broil until top is lightly browned.

THE SKY ROOM HOTEL UTAH

Salt Lake City, Utah, was founded by Mormons seeking a homeplace in which they could freely pursue their chosen religion. No air of religious austerity pervades the beautiful city today. Diners in The Sky Room of the Hotel Utah—owned and operated by the Mormon Church—are treated to magnificent views of the lovely city and of the towering mountains beyond while they enjoy superlative food. Chef Gérard, who learned his distinguished trade in Switzerland and Germany, has supervised The Sky Room's cuisine for nearly thirty years, and takes great pride in his large and varied menus. Some three thousand guests are served daily in The Sky Room.

Chef Gérard Chili

Serves 6 to 8

2 pounds ground chuck
2 tablespoons shortening
1 clove garlic, chopped
1 large onion, chopped
1 can (1 pound) kidney beans
1 can (1 pound) tomatoes, undrained
2 tablespoons chili powder
1 can (10¾ ounces) condensed Cheddar
cheese soup

Brown chuck in shortening until crumbly. Add garlic and onions and sauté until onions are wilted. Pour off excess fat. Add kidney beans, tomatoes, chili powder, and cheese soup. Simmer, stirring occasionally, until chili becomes thick, about 30 minutes.

Chef Gérard Special Potted Lamb

Serves 6

1 boneless leg of lamb, about 3 pounds
¼ cup butter
1 can (10½ ounces) condensed onion soup

1 can (11 ounces) condensed bisque of tomato soup
2 teaspoons caraway seeds
2 tablespoons chopped parsley
½ cup water

Brown lamb in butter in a Dutch oven on all sides. Add remaining ingredients, cover and simmer for 1½ to 2 hours or until lamb is tender. Stir occasionally and turn meat in sauce. Skim excess fat. Slice meat and serve with pan juices.

Velouté Sauce

¼ cup butter or chicken fat (for fish use butter,
for chicken use chicken fat)
¼ cup flour
1 can (10½ ounces) condensed beef broth
1 soup can water
2 peppercorns
1 tablespoon minced parsley
⅛ teaspoon ground nutmeg

Melt butter and stir in flour. Gradually stir in broth. Add remaining ingredients. Simmer, stirring, for 20 minutes. Strain. Can be used as a base sauce for the addition of many other ingredients to make a variety of sauces. Makes about 2½ cups of sauce.

Adaptations from recipes by Chef Gérard.

TRADER VIC'S

From the hilltops of San Francisco one can see so far out over the Pacific that the islands of the South Seas seem to be just over the horizon. It's a beguiling illusion—and one that can be kept alive by a visit to Trader Vic's, where the spell of those islands is marvelously recreated by a menu that draws from the native specialties of such exotic places as Java and Tahiti, China and Japan. The restaurant is owned and operated by Victor Bergeron, known internationally as "Trader Vic," who has collected his recipes for unique food and drink during his extensive travels around the world.

Sukiyaki
Serves 4 to 5

4 medium carrots, cut in thin strips
2 medium onions, thinly sliced
2 bunches green onions, diagonally sliced in
1-inch pieces
2 cups celery, diagonally sliced in ½-inch pieces
1 cup sliced fresh mushrooms (about 4 ounces)
2 cans (5 ounces each) sliced bamboo
shoots, drained
Salad oil
2 pounds sirloin, sliced very thin
¼ pound silver noodles (bean threads), soaked in
warm water, cut in 3-inch pieces
2 squares tofu (bean curd) cut into 12 cubes (optional)
4 cups spinach torn in pieces (about 4 ounces)

Sauce
1 can (10½ ounces) condensed chicken broth
1 cup soy sauce
¼ cup sugar
3 tablespoons sherry

Divide first 6 ingredients in half. Add each in order listed to 2 large skillets and cook in oil until just tender. Push vegetables to one side; divide the meat between the 2 skillets and brown on both sides. Prepare sauce by combining all ingredients; stir 1 cup sauce into each skillet; divide and add noodles and tofu; top with spinach. Cook 5 minutes. Serve Sukiyaki with rice and remaining sauce.

Bean Sprouts with Mushrooms and Celery
Serves 8

¼ cup peanut oil
1 cup sliced celery
2 small onions, sliced
12 small mushrooms, sliced
1 can (10½ ounces) condensed chicken broth
2 tablespoons soy sauce
1 teaspoon MSG
2 cans (16 ounces each) bean sprouts, drained
1 tablespoon cornstarch
¼ cup cold water

Heat peanut oil in a skillet and sauté celery, onions, and mushrooms until wilted. Add chicken broth, soy sauce, and MSG. Add bean sprouts, bring to a boil and boil for 1 minute. Mix cornstarch and water. Stir mixture quickly into bean sprouts. Cook, stirring, until broth bubbles and thickens.

Left: Sukiyaki

Adapted by Owner Trader Vic.

Pota U.S.A. Style

Serves 4 to 6

¼ cup diced salt pork
½ cup chopped cooked chicken
5 cups coarsely chopped Swiss chard leaves or
green part of bok choy
¼ cup chopped green onions
1 can (10½ ounces) condensed chicken broth
½ teaspoon MSG
Juice of ½ lemon
½ cup hot light cream
¼ cup shredded coconut
2 tablespoons cornstarch
¼ cup cold water

Sauté salt pork until brown. Stir in chicken, Swiss chard, and green onions. Add broth, MSG, and lemon juice. Simmer, covered, until chard is tender, about 10 minutes. Pour cream over coconut and let stand until cool. Strain, pressing all cream from coconut. Pour coconut cream into chard mixture. Mix cornstarch and water, stir mixture into chard. Cook, stirring, until sauce bubbles and thickens.

Baked Chicken Cashew

Serves 4

2 whole chicken breasts, about 1½ pounds, split
4 chicken thighs, about 1 pound
2 tablespoons salad oil
2 tablespoons butter or margarine
2 tablespoons brandy
1 can (10½ ounces) condensed cream of chicken soup
⅓ cup sour cream
1 tablespoon chopped onion
½ teaspoon paprika
Generous dash pepper
½ teaspoon MSG
½ cup coarsely chopped cashews

In skillet, brown chicken in oil and butter; pour off fat. Remove chicken. Add brandy; stir to loosen browned bits. Blend in remaining ingredients except cashews; add chicken. Cover; cook over low heat 45 minutes, stirring now and then. Add cashews; cook 15 minutes more. Cook uncovered to thicken the sauce, if desired.

Chicken and Bananas

Serves 6

3 broiler-fryers, quartered
Salt, pepper
½ cup peanut oil
Nutmeg
12 ti leaves (optional)

144

3 cans (10½ ounces each) condensed chicken broth
12 bananas, peeled and halved lengthwise
¾ cup butter

Sprinkle chicken with salt and pepper. Sauté chicken in oil until golden brown on all sides. Sprinkle chicken very lightly with nutmeg. Place chicken pieces, 2 to a portion, in individual casseroles. If you have ti leaves line the casseroles with the leaves. Pour ½ can chicken broth over each chicken portion. Sauté bananas in butter for 2 minutes. Place bananas over chicken pieces. Fold over ti leaves to enclose chicken and bananas; then cover casserole with foil. Bake in a preheated 350°F. oven for 40 to 45 minutes or until the chicken is tender.

Rumaki

Makes about 36 canapés

1 tablespoon sugar
1 large bay leaf
Dash ground cinnamon
1 can (10½ ounces) condensed chicken broth
2 teaspoons grated fresh ginger root
1 tablespoon anise seed
1 clove garlic, crushed
⅔ cup Japanese soy sauce
1 pound chicken livers
1 can (5 ounces) water chestnuts, drained
½ pound sliced bacon

In a bowl combine sugar, bay leaf, cinnamon, chicken broth, ginger root, anise seed, garlic, and soy sauce. Cut each chicken liver in half. Cut each water chestnut into quarters, dividing them crosswise into slices. Cut each bacon slice into thirds. Wrap bacon slice around 1 chicken liver half and 1 slice water chestnut. Fasten with a toothpick. Place in chicken broth mixture. Let marinate for 1 hour or longer. Drain and broil until bacon is crisp and livers are done. Serve the Rumaki hot.

Chinese Watercress Soup

Serves 4 to 6

1 bunch watercress
¼ pound lean pork, finely diced
1 teaspoon cornstarch
1 teaspoon salt
½ teaspoon pepper
¼ teaspoon sugar
½ teaspoon grated fresh ginger root
1 tablespoon soy sauce
1 tablespoon peanut oil
2 cans (10½ ounces each) condensed chicken broth
2 cups water

Wash watercress and trim heavy stems. Chop watercress finely. Mix pork, cornstarch, salt, pepper, sugar, ginger root, and soy sauce. Heat oil and brown pork mixture. Add chicken broth and water and bring to a boil; simmer 10 minutes. Add watercress and simmer another 5 minutes.

Poi Stew

Serves 4

1½ pounds potatoes or taro root
½-inch-thick slice top round (1½ pounds)
½ pound mushrooms, sliced
1½ tablespoons oil
¼ cup chopped scallions
1 can (10½ ounces) condensed chicken broth
¾ cup water
¼ cup soy sauce
1½ teaspoons MSG
Salt
2 tablespoons cornstarch
¼ cup cold water

Scrub potatoes. Cover with water and boil until tender. Drain, peel, and cut into ¾-inch cubes. Pound round steak until paper thin. Cut steak into strips ¾ inch wide and 3 inches long. Sauté beef and mushrooms in oil until beef is just cooked. Add scallions, chicken broth, water, soy sauce, and MSG. Cover and cook for 5 minutes. Fold in potatoes. Season to taste with salt. Mix cornstarch and water and stir into meat mixture. Cook, stirring, until mixture bubbles and thickens.

Mock Bird's Nest Soup

Serves 6 to 8

1 bundle long rice or 1 cup uncooked fine egg noodles
2 cans (10½ ounces each) condensed chicken broth
4 large mushrooms, chopped
½ teaspoon MSG
1 cup minced fresh lean pork
1 cup finely chopped smoked ham
½ cup chopped water chestnuts
2 egg whites, slightly beaten
1 tablespoon chopped Chinese parsley or parsley

If long rice is used cut into ¼-inch lengths and soak in hot water 30 minutes. Heat chicken broth, adding 2½ cups water to the broth. Add mushrooms, MSG, pork, ham, and water chestnuts. Drain long rice and add to soup. Bring to a boil and simmer 10 minutes. (If you are using fine noodles just add them as they are to soup, cook about 10 minutes, until tender.) Stir egg whites into broth. Simmer 5 minutes. Garnish each serving with chopped parsley.

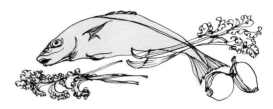

Fish Baked in Ti Leaves

Serves 6

1 sea bass or red snapper, about 5 pounds,
cleaned and scaled
1 teaspoon salt
1 tablespoon minced onion
1 teaspoon minced parsley
¼ cup minced celery
2 tablespoons melted butter
½ teaspoon salt
¼ teaspoon paprika
¼ teaspoon pepper
½ teaspoon dill seed
2 cups ½-inch bread cubes
1 can (10½ ounces) condensed chicken broth
Ti leaves (optional)
1 lemon, sliced
2 ounces salt pork, cut into thin strips

Wash bass and pat dry. Rub inside and out with salt. Combine onion, parsley, celery, butter, salt, paprika, pepper, dill seed, bread cubes, and ½ cup chicken broth. Blend well and use mixture to stuff fish. Sew or skewer opening. Place fish in pan lined with ti leaves or foil. Top fish with lemon slices, salt pork, and the remainder of chicken broth. Wrap ti leaves over fish or enclose in foil, sealing tightly. Bake in a preheated 350°F. oven for 1 to 1½ hours or until fish flakes easily. Place fish on a platter. Garnish with watercress sprigs and lemon slices, cutting the fish into crosswise slices to serve.

Swiss Hütte

After a day on the slopes, no skier asks more of life than to settle down in a firelit room while he warms himself with hot buttered rum and lingers over a menu laden with Middle-European gourmet delights. The Swiss Hütte in Hillsdale, New York, provides delicious food, fine lodging—and more, during the summer, when dinner is served out-of-doors in a garden surrounded by panoramic mountain views.

Geschnitzeltes Kalbfleisch
Veal in White Wine and Cream
Serves 4

1½ *pounds veal cut from round*
¼ *cup butter*
1 *cup dry white wine*
1 *can (10½ ounces) condensed cream of potato soup*
⅓ *cup light cream*
1 *tablespoon lemon juice*
2 *tablespoons chopped parsley*

Slice veal into strips ¼ inch wide and 2 inches in length. Sauté veal in butter until golden brown. Add white wine and simmer until wine is almost absorbed. Press soup through a sieve and stir soup and cream into veal. Simmer until veal is tender. Stir in lemon juice and parsley. Serve with Roesti Potatoes.

Roesti Potatoes
4 *medium Idaho potatoes*
½ *cup butter*

Cover potatoes with water and boil until potatoes are easily pierced but still firm. Peel and grate on a coarse grater. Shape potatoes into 4 large cakes. Sprinkle with salt and pepper on both sides. Fry cakes in butter until richly browned and crusty on both sides.

Adaptations from recipes by Owners Linda and Tom Breen.

Sweetbreads and Lobster Poulette Sauce
Serves 4

2 *pairs sweetbreads*
Water
1 *tablespoon lemon juice*
1 *teaspoon salt*
1½ *cups fresh, frozen, or canned*
lobster meat
⅓ *cup butter*
3 *egg yolks*
1 *tablespoon cornstarch*
1 *tablespoon lemon juice*
1 *can (10¼ ounces) condensed oyster stew*
1 *can (10 ½ ounces) condensed*
chicken broth

Cover sweetbreads with water. Add lemon juice and salt; simmer for 10 minutes. Drop sweetbreads into cold water. Remove membranes and slice sweetbreads. Sauté sweetbreads and lobster in hot butter for 2 minutes. Keep warm. In another saucepan combine egg yolks, cornstarch, and lemon juice. Stir in oyster stew and chicken broth. Cook over low heat, stirring constantly, until sauce bubbles and thickens. Pour sauce over sweetbreads and lobster. Reheat; do not boil.

Sun Valley Lodge

Warmed by a sun that sparkles on snowfields in winter and brightens the brilliant green of summer, Sun Valley, one of the most famous resorts in the world, nestles in a bowl-shaped valley in the Sawtooth Mountains of Idaho. Although noted for its skiing, the resort boasts year-round attractions and visitors flock to its entertainments in all seasons. In winter skating and sleigh rides provide activities for those who find skiing too strenuous. There is swimming—in two enclosed warm-water pools—and ice skating all year, as well as indoor bowling, movies, and dancing. When the weather is warm, fishing, tennis, golf, riding, and skeet and trap shooting are the chief attractions. In short, Sun Valley has something for everyone. Sumptuous food, eaten before a blazing fire at Sun Valley Lodge, has become a tradition. The Lodge offers visitors all the amenities, along with a varied menu of delicious and substantial food geared to outdoors-sharpened appetites. Diners may be served in front of a blazing fire.

Stuffed Cabbage, Dutch Style

Serves 6

1 pound ground chuck
½ pound ground raw pork
1½ cups cooked rice
1 medium onion, chopped
⅛ teaspoon each thyme, paprika, sage, pepper
1½ teaspoons salt
¼ teaspoon ground caraway
12 large leaves green cabbage (do not use tough outer leaves)
2 cans (10¾ ounces each) condensed tomato soup

Combine chuck, pork, rice, onion, spices, salt, and caraway. Drop 12 cabbage leaves into boiling salted water and simmer for 5 minutes. Drain and cool. Divide meat mixture among leaves and roll up so that cabbage completely encloses meat. Place rolls side by side in a single layer in a 9- x 13-inch pan. Cover with the tomato soup. Cover pan and bake in a preheated 350°F. oven for about 1 hour or until the cabbage is tender.

El Torito's Salsa Picante

Piquant Sauce

3 cups "V-8" juice
2 cans (11 ounces each) condensed bisque of tomato soup
2 tablespoons meat concentrate
2 to 4 cloves garlic, minced
1 cup chopped green onions
2 tablespoons minced green chilies
Salt

Blend ingredients in a large saucepan and bring to a boil. Simmer, stirring occasionally, for 20 minutes or until onion is tender. Spoon over spaghetti, chicken, noodles, rice, omelette, shrimp, veal, meat loaf, or pork chops. This sauce can also be used in preparing a meat loaf. Sauce can be made ahead and frozen in portion-size batches. Makes about 7 cups of sauce.

Adapted by Chef Fred Highbee.

THE Sea Gull

Gulls fly low over Lake Michigan at the foot of Chicago's East Randolph Street, and as you walk into The Sea Gull you might well be entering the dining salon of a luxury liner. A handsome restaurant of subdued elegance, the décor of The Sea Gull is maritime, and so is its extensive menu. The Sea Gull is open only for dinner.

Brook Trout Stuffed with Crab Meat

Serves 6

¼ cup butter
½ cup flour
2 cans (10 ounces each) frozen condensed oyster stew, thawed
1 egg yolk
2 tablespoons butter
2 teaspoons minced shallots or white onions
¼ cup minced fresh mushrooms
2 teaspoons minced parsley
3 tablespoons white wine
½ pound crab meat
6 trout, split and boned
Salt, pepper
Flour
¾ cup butter
Lemon wedges

Melt ¼ cup butter and stir in flour. Stir in oyster stew. Cook over low heat, stirring, until sauce bubbles and thickens. Beat in egg yolk. Set aside. Melt 2 tablespoons butter; sauté shallots, mushrooms, and parsley until soft, about 5 minutes. Stir in wine. Cook at a boil until wine evaporates. Stir in crab meat and oyster sauce. Keep hot over very low heat. Sprinkle trout inside and out with salt and pepper. Roll trout in flour. Melt ¾ cup butter and spoon half of the butter over the bottom of a shallow baking pan; arrange trout in the pan in a single layer. Bake in a preheated 350°F. oven for 20 to 25 minutes or until trout are cooked. Carefully open trout and fill with crab meat stuffing. Close trout. Heat remaining butter until golden brown and spoon over filled trout. Reheat in oven 5 minutes. Serve with lemon wedges.

Italian Tomato Sauce

¼ cup olive oil
2 large onions, minced
2 cloves garlic, minced
1 can (11 ounces) condensed bisque of tomato soup
2 cups country-style tomato juice
2 bay leaves
⅓ cup minced parsley
¼ teaspoon oregano
1 piece lemon peel, 1 x 4 inches
⅓ cup dry white wine
2 tablespoons Worcestershire sauce
Salt, freshly ground black pepper

Heat olive oil and sauté onions and garlic until golden. Add soup, juice, bay leaves, parsley, oregano, lemon peel, white wine, Worcestershire. Simmer for 30 minutes, stirring occasionally. Season to taste with salt and pepper. Remove bay leaves and lemon peel. Serve with any bland dish, such as pasta, veal, fish steaks, omelet, etc. Makes 1 quart of sauce.

Adapted from recipes by Chef Werner Heil.

Named for Louis IX of France, the city of St. Louis grew on the site of a fur-trading post. The early settlers were French, followed by a migration of Germans in the mid-1800's. Today, St. Louis is a bustling, cosmopolitan city, the second largest land transportation center in the nation. Forest Park, the Jefferson National Memorial, and the beautiful Byzantine St. Louis Cathedral are among the many attractions of this modern, constantly expanding city and well worth the visitor's attention. Following a day of sight-seeing, Tony's is an ideal choice for a satisfying Italian dinner. After the death of their father, some twenty years ago, the Bommarito brothers took over his tavern-restaurant and made it an award-winning dining place.

Tenderloin Marsala alla Tony's

Serves 4

1 cup green pepper strips
1½ cups sliced fresh mushrooms
4 shallots, minced, or ¼ cup minced green onions
¼ cup olive oil
8 beef tenderloin slices, 4 ounces each
Salt, pepper
1 can (10½ ounces) condensed beef broth
¼ cup Marsala wine
2 teaspoons cornstarch (optional)
¼ cup water (optional)

Sauté green peppers, mushrooms, and shallots in olive oil. Remove vegetables when tender. Sprinkle beef with salt and pepper. Sauté beef slices in pan drippings until just brown on both sides. Pour off excess fat. Add vegetables, beef broth, and Marsala. Simmer for 5 minutes. Thicken, if desired, by mixing cornstarch with water and stirring quickly into broth. Cook, stirring, until sauce bubbles and thickens. Serve with buttered pasta, a tossed green salad with olive oil and vinegar dressing, and a robust red wine to round out a hearty, savory dinner.

Chicken alla Crema alla Tony's

Serves 4

2 chicken breasts, split
Salt, pepper
⅓ cup butter
1½ cups sliced fresh mushrooms
¼ cup white Burgundy wine
2 tablespoons orange juice
1 teaspoon grated orange rind
1 can (10½ ounces) condensed cream of chicken soup

Remove skin and bones from chicken breasts. Sprinkle chicken with salt and pepper. Heat butter in a skillet and brown chicken quickly on both sides. Add mushrooms and sauté until mushrooms wilt. Add remaining ingredients and simmer until chicken is cooked, about 15 minutes. Serve with risotto and a marinated artichoke hearts salad. A light chilled white wine such as Soave would be the perfect accompaniment.

Adapted by Owner-Chef Vincent J. Bommarito.

MENU FRENCH, MENU ITALIAN

This glossary is intended to guide the reader through French and Italian menus. It lays no claim to completeness, but it does cover familiar dishes, and quite a few that are often served but are less familiar.

Both French and Italian cuisine differ regionally; hence, the profusion of regional and city names. The French have immortalized their great chefs by naming certain dishes (especially sauces) after them. For example, the Marquis de Béchamel, who is said to have created the famous Béchamel sauce, was the maître d'hôtel of Louis XIV. On the other hand, French terms such as "à la reine" and "suprême" are nowadays used loosely, and do not specifically connote "to the Queen's taste" or "superb."

Most Italian menus combine Italian and English and very few French menus are in French only. Those menus entirely in Italian usually present English alongside.

In any event, with the help of this glossary, any reader should be able to select a fine meal without those unexpected misunderstandings.

FRENCH

agneau—lamb (see also *côte d'agneau, gigot d'agneau*)

à la, au, aux—in the style of, with, or in (regional variations)

à la carte—choice of individual dishes, as distinguished from complete menu (see *table d'hôte*)

à l'ancienne—old style, mostly with rice, Béchamel sauce, mushrooms (see *Béchamel, sauce*)

à la crème—with cream

à la mode—mostly, *boeuf à la mode* (beef, home style); but: *tripes à la mode de Caen,* or tripe Caen (Normandy) style

à la reine—in queenly style; elaborate; often used with *oeufs* (eggs) or *potage* (soup)

amandine—slivered, buttered almonds (see *filet de sole amandine*)

artichaut—artichoke (see *fond*)

asperges—asparagus

assiette anglaise—assorted cold cuts

au beurre—with butter

au citron—with lemon

au gratin—sprinkled with crumbs, sometimes cheese, baked brown

au jus—with natural gravy

au lait—with milk; e.g., *café au lait*

au vin—with wine (see *coq au vin*)

aux champignons—with mushrooms; e.g., *omelette aux champignons*

Béarnaise, sauce—made of egg yolks, wine, vinegar, and herbs, often served with tenderloin steak (also see *tournedos*)

Béchamel, sauce—made of chicken stock, cream, flour, butter, seasoned with onions

bisque—rich cream soup, generally made with seafood

blanquette de veau—veal stew with white sauce and rice (see *veau*)

boeuf à la mode—beef, home style

————**bouilli**—boiled beef

————**Bourguignon**—with Burgundy wine, shallots, and mushrooms

————**braisé**—braised beef

————**daube glacé**—spiced beef stew with vegetables, often in aspic

bombe—ice cream dessert in mold

bonne femme—plain, home style (see *filet de sole bonne femme*)

Bordelaise, sauce—made of meat stock, various seasonings, often with red wine

bouillabaisse—Mediterranean fish stew or soup, Marseilles specialty

bouillon—clear beef stock

café arrosé—coffee laced with brandy

————**noir**—black coffee

canard—duck

————**à l'orange**—with orange, sometimes flavored with liqueur

carottes—carrots

cassoulet—baked white kidney beans with pork, goose, or duck meat

champignons—mushrooms

Chantilly—with sweetened, flavored whipped cream

chasseur—hunter style, with wine, mushrooms, shallots, and herbs

Châteaubriand—thickest cut of tenderloin beef

choucroute—sauerkraut

choucroute garnie—pickled cabbage with pork or frankfurters

chou-fleur—cauliflower

choux de Bruxelles—Brussels sprouts

compote de fruits—mixed stewed fruits

consommé—clear broth, mostly beef

————**Madrilène**—Madrid style, with tomatoes; often served cold in aspic

coq au vin—fowl cooked in wine

coquille St. Jacques—various seafoods (often scallops) prepared with parsley butter or cream sauce, served in shell

côte d'agneau—lamb chop

côtelette—cutlet, chop; e.g., *côtelette de veau*

crème caramel—caramel custard

————**de marrons**—sweetened chestnut purée (see *marrons*)

crêpes—plain thin pancakes
_____Suzette—very thin pancakes, flavored with orange, lemon, or curaçao, flamed with brandy
crevettes—shrimp
croquettes—patties of chopped food
croûtons—small cubes of toasted or fried bread

Duchesse—potatoes mashed with beaten egg yolks; e.g., *pommes Duchesse* (see *pommes*)

émincé—minced
en brochette—on a skewer or spit
en cocotte—served in a covered casserole
en coquille—served in shell
en papillote—baked in oiled paper bag or aluminum foil
entrée—main course of meal
entremets—any kind of side dishes (vegetables, salads, etc.)
épinards—spinach
escalope—thin slice of meat, mostly veal; e.g., *escalope de veau*
escargots—snails

faisan—pheasant
filet de sole amandine—fillet of sole with slivered, buttered almonds
_____bonne femme—plain, home style
_____meunière—with browned butter, lemon juice, and chopped parsley
fines herbes—mixture of minced herbs; e.g., *omelette aux fines herbes*
flambé—flamed; e.g. *pêches flambées* (flamed with brandy, kirsch)
flan—baked custard; small pastry with cream or fruit filling
foie—liver; e.g., *pâté de foie* gras (see *gras* and *pâté*)
fond—mostly, heart; e.g., *fonds d'artichauts*
fondue au fromage—melted cheese dish (see *fromage*)

fraises—strawberries
framboises—raspberries
fricandeau—usually veal in a white sauce
frit—fried, deep fried; e.g., *pommes frites*
fromage—cheese

gigot d'agneau—leg of lamb
glacé—iced; e.g., *marrons glacés*
gras—fat; e.g., *pâté de foie gras* (goose liver pâté)

haché—finely chopped
haricots verts—green beans
Hollandaise, sauce—made of butter, eggs, and lemon juice
homard—lobster
hors d'oeuvre—appetizers
huîtres—oysters

jambon—ham
jardinière—diced, mixed vegetables
julienne—thin strips of vegetable, meat, or cheese; e.g., *potage julienne* (see *potage*)

laitue—lettuce
langue—tongue; e.g., *langue de boeuf*

macédoine—mixed vegetables or fruits
marrons—chestnuts
médaillon—round-shaped piece of meat, usually beef
meunière, sauce—made of browned butter, lemon, chopped parsley, usually served with fish; e.g., *filet de sole meunière*
mignon—choice filet of beef
mille-feuilles—delicate French pastry
Mornay, sauce—white, with sharp cheese and egg yolks
moules—mussels, often served with *sauce ravigote* (see *ravigote*)
mousse—mostly, fluffy dessert, e.g., *mousse au chocolat*

pain—bread
pâté—finely ground mixture of meat or poultry, often liver
pêches—peaches
perdrix—partridge
petite marmite—classic French meat-vegetable soup
petits pois—tiny peas
pintade—guinea hen
poires—pears
poisson—fish
poitrine de capon—breast of capon
pommes—apples; also abb. of *pommes de terre* (potatoes)
porc—pork
potage—soup
_____St. Germain—made of split peas, crumbled bacon, cheese, with croutons
pot-au-feu—classic French meat-and-vegetable stew
poularde, poulet—chicken
printanière—with spring vegetables
purée—mashed; e.g., *pommes purées*

quenelles—small dumplings made of finely ground meat or fish
_____de brochet—pike dumplings
quiche Lorraine—open custard cheese pie, usually with chopped bacon

ravigote, sauce—served cold, made of vinegar, oil, chopped onions, hard-cooked eggs, herbs; often served with seafoods
riz—rice
rognons—kidneys
rôti—roast (meats, etc.)
roulade—rolled veal or beef

soubise, sauce—white, with onions sometimes parsley, often served with lamb
soufflé—baked fluffy main dish or dessert
soupe—soup
_____à l'oignon—French onion soup
_____du jour—available on a given day

sous cloche—under glass

Suédoise—Swedish style

suprême—the most delicate portion of meat, poultry; sometimes refers to delicate desserts

suprême de volaille—breast of chicken (see *volaille*)

suprême, sauce—rich, creamy sauce

table d'hôte—complete meal at a fixed price, as distinguished from *à la carte*

tournedos—choice filets of beef, usually served with *sauce Béarnaise*

tripes à la mode de Caen—tripe Caen style, cooked in apple cider, or white wine and brandy

truffles—truffles; edible fungus of the mushroom family; exquisite flavoring for many dishes (meat, fowl, game, etc.)

veau—veal

velouté—thick, creamy sauce or soup; e.g., *velouté d'asperges*

vichyssoise—creamy soup of puréed potatoes, chicken stock, and leeks; best served cold

vinaigrette—sauce made of oil, vinegar, pepper, and herbs; e.g., *asperges vinaigrette*

volaille—breast of chicken

vol-au-vent—fluffy pastry, filled with meat, poultry, or seafood in rich cream sauce

ITALIAN

agnelotti—lamb patties cooked with cheese and wine

al dente—correct way of cooking pasta products, firm, never overcooked (also see *pasta*)

alla, alle, all'—in the style of, with, or in; e.g., *alla Milanese*—Milan style

antipasto or **antipasti**—assorted cold cuts and other appetizers

bagna cauda—sauce (mainly anchovies, garlic, mushrooms), served with certain vegetables

biscotti—cookies

cacciatore—sautéed with mushrooms and onions; e.g., *veal cacciatore*

canneloni—hollow macaroni or rolled pancakes, filled with cheese, fish, meat, or mushrooms

cappucino—coffee with hot milk, sometimes sprinkled with cinnamon

cassata—frozen dessert, usually combining cream, ice cream, cake

confettura—confection

costoletta di vitella—veal chop or cutlet (also see *vitella*)

fagioli—beans

fegato di vitella—calf liver

fettucine—egg noodles in various styles; e.g., *alla papalina*, with ham and butter

formaggio—cheese (Italian varieties)

Fra Diavolo—spicy tomato sauce (named after famous local bandit)

frutti di mare—mixed seafood

funghi—mushrooms; usually *con* (with) *funghi*

gamberetti—small shrimp

gelati—ice creams (also see *spumone, tortone*)

inglese—English style; usually with all' (all'inglese); used with *steak*, it means *rare*

insalata verde—green salad

lasagne—broad flat noodles

maccheroni—macaroni

manicotti—large pasta filled with cheese

marinara—tomato and garlic sauce with clams and mussels, sailor style

Milanese—Milan style (breaded, fried, with Parmesan cheese)

minestrone—thick soup, varying according to region

mortadella—cooked sausage, basically of spiced pork

osso buco—slices of braised veal shank in tomato sauce

pane—bread

parmigiano—Parmesan cheese, dishes made with it, e.g., *veal Parmigiana*

pasta—all forms of spaghetti or similar foods

peperoni—peppers, prepared in various ways; e.g., *arrostiti* (roasted)

pizza—flat pie filled with cheese and tomatoes

polenta—cornmeal pudding

pollo—chicken, prepared in various ways; e.g., *arrosto* (roasted)

prosciutto—dark smoked ham

ravioli—squares of pasta filled with minced meat, spinach, or cheese

risotto—rice cooked in stock and oil, with regional variations

saltimbocca—slices of veal fried with ham, sage, and cheese, dash of Marsala wine

scaloppine—thin slices of boneless veal, prepared in various ways; e.g., *scaloppine limone*—veal with lemon butter

scampi—large shrimp

spumone—layers of ice cream with candied fruit

tortone—frozen cream with crushed macaroons

vitella—veal

zabaglione—egg yolks beaten in Marsala wine, sometimes rum

zucchini—long green squash

zuppa—soup; but *zuppa inglese*—rich rum cake topped with whipped cream

TABLE SETTINGS

All the restaurants in this book are top-flight for more reasons than their food. In surroundings and décor they establish a mood; their service is gracious and meticulously correct; their tables are set with charm and elegance, and the prisms on their chandeliers would crack in chagrin if ever a diner had to say, however quietly, "May I have another fork, please."

There is no reason why this same glamour and elegance, this same air of gracious expertise, can't be transferred to the home—for everyday as well as for special occasions. Let your credo be to set tables with a difference. Yet extraordinary tables need not be—should not be—fussy time-consuming affairs. The important ingredient is flair.

Indeed, whatever enhances, whatever is appealing, is *right* for setting a table; there are no longer the strict rules that Emily Post once laid down and every right-thinking hostess made a point of adhering to slavishly.

First, **to cover the table,** you might ask yourself whether it is necessary to cover it at all; the gleam of polished wood or the sparkle of glass can be a very handsome "tablecloth" in itself. However, almost anything that looks attractive is appropriate. If you have a cherished lace tablecloth, bring it up to date with an underskirt of bright hue to show through the pattern—it could be a colored sheet, two stitched-together lengths of felt, or a dress fabric in just the shade you want.

Indeed, all sorts of fabrics that certainly can't be called "table linen" can be turned into lovely **tablecloths.** Yard goods found in the up-holstery department, for example. Felt as the tablecloth itself, rather than as an under-cloth, for it comes in a wide range of enchanting, vibrant colors. Perhaps an India print that you had first considered as a wall-hanging can be second-guessed as a tablecloth. Bedspreads make wonderful coverings for the table. The rich patterns and unusual color combinations of by-the-yard terry cloth make a different dress for an informal table.

Think of this: for this particular dinner, would a number of small tables serve the purpose better? Perhaps the **dining-room table** can go back against the wall to do duty as a buffet or a large, accommodating server. The guests can be seated at **small tables** nearby, with the living room and/or hall pressed into service if need be. Card tables are easy to come by—borrow as many as you'll need. Dress them all alike or each one different from all the others, as the mood seizes you. If the dinner has a formal flavor, you might make sheer tablecloths of white organdy or organza or *peau de soie,* and give each an underskirt of a different, subtle color. If the mood is less formal, how about beach towels in a riot of colors and patterns?

Place mats have been with us for quite a while: have you ever stopped to consider the changes that can be rung on these serviceable items? Foreign-import stores, or such departments in department stores, often yield exciting discoveries for this purpose—small, colorful **runners** or mats, meant to protect a living-room table from the base of a lamp or vase, can do double duty as place mats. The small **lacquer trays,** in glorious colors, found in oriental import shops, make wonderful backdrops for dishes and utensils chosen with flair. Or do-it-yourself with handsome place mats cut from a roll of really beautiful, heavy—perhaps embossed or flocked—wallpaper. Going even farther afield, how about a handsome obi—the sash the Japanese wear about the waists of their kimonos—pressed into service as a runner? (You'll see one used this way in one of the color pictures in this book. Indeed, a study of the props used in the color photography in this book will profit anyone interested in inventive table setting. In these unique pictures you will discover a host of unusual decorative accessories used in unusual ways.)

Of course there must be **napkins**—or, at least, something that serves the purpose. These can match the tablecloth if you feel traditional, contrast with it if you feel experimental. Fingertip towels make excellent napkins; terry fingertip towels are nothing short of a blessing if the menu includes hard-to-manage foods.

Tradition says that the **centerpiece** for the table will be an arrangement of flowers—low enough so that guests can see each other across the table—flanked by candles. Tradition has long ago gone by the boards and, in most cases, that's all to the good. **Flowers?** By all means—if you want them. But if you do, how about a small nosegay at each place, in an appropriate small container, such as a glass made for a votive candle or a bud vase or a pretty teacup? How about a chain of daisies or clover—remember how you made such chains when you were a child?—down the length of the table? How about single blossoms floated in a circle of small, shallow bowls?

If you'd prefer flowers in the living room but none for dining, try one of a dozen other possible somethings to decorate your table. Nearest to flowers is **greenery**—masses or garlands of leaves or small branches make lovely patterns, in their own way as beautiful as flowers, if a bit more subtle. Or use the greens as a foundation for an entirely different concept. Try setting a whole colony of miniature dolls in the greens. Or a jumble of

balls of many colors and sizes. Or a clutch of ivory or alabaster eggs. Or a garden of porcelain or silk or bead flowers. Or use greens to house a farmyard or a jungle of small porcelain or glass animals. If you're a collector—snuffboxes? figurines? owls? patch or stamp boxes? whatever!—tuck your collection among the greens for a unique display.

What else makes a centerpiece? **Fruit. Vegetables.** One of the handsomest things in the world is a plump eggplant, its purple skin wiped with an oil-dampened cloth so that it glistens sleekly. Multiply that by four or five or six, gracing, say, a shallow brass bowl, and you couldn't ask for a more regal elegance. Peppers—red ones, green ones, long pale chartreuse ones—are handsome in shape, convenient in size to make a wreath or cluster in a bowl. Fill a shallow dish with the intense green of limes or the bright yellow of lemons, or set them three at a time, piled tepee-style, in a half dozen pewter porringers. Do a little apple-polishing and pile the fruit in a wooden trencher, or grandmother's black iron "spider," filling in the spaces between with portly brown walnuts. Arrange a careful pyramid of tangerines and tuck lemon leaves, a leaf at a time, in the interstices.

Now, about those **candles.** We all know that everything—the people, the food, the table—looks better by candlelight. But that doesn't necessarily mean two candles or four or six, like soldiers on guard, flanking a centerpiece. You might try a candle at each place setting. There are available small holders that take a candle in the center, with room for a pretty circle of flowers around it—and there you are, flowers and candles in one.

A last word, this time not about table settings, but the more prosaic business of setting the table. The watchword: do it early. Do some of it the night before if you can—if you worry about dust, throw a sheet over the table until the next day. Arrange the flowers or fruit or whatever will be your decoration early, too, and set it all in place. Have the candles arranged, ready to light. Have, insofar as possible, no last-minute worries. A serene hostess enjoys her own party—and when she does, so do her guests.

154

Index

155

156